BEING
BEYOND
BELIEF

Is it time to turn your world
Inside out and upside down
To release that joy from your heart
You've been too long with that frown

Is it time to turn your thinking
On it's head so you can start
To see what's real and true for you
Some say that's called 'smart'!

BEING BEYOND BELIEF

Mike George

Text Copyright Mike George 2017

Print Edition ISBN: 978-0-9933877-2-2

Also available as an E-Book

First published by Gavisus Media 2017
Email: gavisusmedia@gmail.com
Second Edition
The moral rights of the author have been asserted.

Cover Design: Charlotte Mouncey - www.bookstyle.co.uk

The information given in this book should not be treated as a substitute for professional medical advice; always consult a medical practitioner. Any use of information in this book is at the reader's discretion and risk. Neither the author nor the publisher can be held responsible for any loss, claim or damage arising out of use, or misuse, or the suggestions made or the failure to take medical advice

Other Books by Mike George

MINDSETS
Changing your perception
and creating new perspectives

The 7 Myths About LOVE...Actually!
The Journey from Your HEAD
to the HEART of Your SOUL

BEING Your Self
SEEing and KNOWing
What's IN the Way IS the Way!

Don't Get MAD Get Wise
Why no one ever makes you angry...ever!

The Immune System of the SOUL
Freeing Your Self from ALL Forms of Dis - ease

The Journey from IGNORANCE to ENIGHTENMENT
The only journey where you are guaranteed
to lose all your baggage.

The 7 AHA!s of Highly Enlightened Souls
How to Free YOUR Self from ALL Forms of Stress

Learn to Find Inner Peace
Manage your anxieties, think well, feel well.

Learn to Relax
Ease tension, conquer stress and free the self

In the Light of Meditation
A guide to meditation and spiritual awakening

A Humble Request

Please do not believe a word you read in this book.

If you turn the information in these pages into
more beliefs then you are likely
to become stuck!

It doesn't matter whether you agree with anything or not.

Always ask 'is this true for me' right now.

Use the words and sentences as signposts.
They are recommending that you explore this within
your own consciousness.

Only then can you begin to awaken from the dream that you create
using the beliefs that you either learn from others
or create within your self.

But if you keep filtering life through your beliefs you
may never develop the clarity to know reality.

And not even know you do so.

Only your own quiet, gentle, yet earnestly curious
questioning reveals the deeper truths that you need to know.

CONTENTS

Only beyond <u>belief</u> can you <u>know</u> what is <u>true.</u>

I love you

I love

I

I

I am

I am love

Introduction

Throwing down the Gauntlet to YOU

Yes the subtitle of this book is a little melodramatic. But beliefs can and do kill. Most people who kill other people are driven by their beliefs. That's obvious when you look into the dynamics of any conflict. But what's not so obvious is how your beliefs can kill you.

It's simple! And it goes like this. If you believe, for example, in 'loss', then you will make your self sad whenever what you believe you possessed leaves your life. You will even make your self sad as you watch the others experiencing loss. Sadness then becomes a habit, a permanent cloud within your personality. Sometimes it becomes depression, which then weakens your physical immune system, which allows disease to take over and eventually kill your body.

Yes I know it's a bit simplistic, but follow the trail of any of the three emotional families, sadness, anger or fear, and you will always arrive at how they can affect your physical health. The evidence for the 'psychosomatic effect' is now out there in abundance.

Of course some people of a more spiritual inclination, will say that you don't die, it's just your body that dies. But that's for another chapter!

During the following pages I will attempt to clarify two things. Firstly, that most of the beliefs that we have all learned or absorbed are not true. And until that's realized they will slowly affect our wellbeing and then our health, in detrimental and sometimes fatal ways.

Secondly, as long as you hold on to any belief you may never 'know' what is true. You may believe you know but you don't. As soon as someone says, "I don't know", that is often the beginning of him or her being true to themselves.

Yes that's a big claim. A big belief you may say! But my challenge to you, as I throw down the gauntlet, is not to believe anything I say, but to 'see for your self'.

The Age of Unlearning

I was recently asked in an interview 'what do you mean by unlearning'? My answer is that we are now in the 'age of unlearning' by necessity. To unlearn is to challenge every belief you have been taught or created and to see if it is true for you. It sounds obvious. It even sounds easy. But it's not so obvious for most and it's not so easy.

First we have to become aware of the beliefs that are running our program. This means becoming aware of the beliefs that are the basis of our personality and that emerge continuously in our thoughts, conversations and behaviors. And that level of awareness, in this busy modern world, is not common.

As you read any of the following reflections on what I perceive to be the primary beliefs we have all been misleadingly taught, you may 'occasionally' have the thought, "But these are just Mike's beliefs"! To you, that would 'seem' to be the case. You are taking in the information and then creating new beliefs...possibly. Then perhaps thinking, "Well these are just more beliefs". That's from your point of view. But from my point of view these are things I no longer believe. I've challenged the beliefs, realized and explained why they are not true for me, and headed for the territory called 'knowing'. This is something we can only do for our self.

I am inviting you to do the same, in your own way, in your own time. If you don't then your beliefs may not kill you but they will likely sabotage the wellness of your being and therefore your happiness.

I am basically suggesting that the 30 beliefs that I have identified are not 'accurate representations' of what is true in each area. That said, it could be easily argued that no verbal or written re-presentation is ever true. It is, after all, only a 're-presentation'.

But I cannot 'make' you see that.

Sometimes you will read something and you will say/think to your self, 'yes, I get that, I know that's true, or at least more accurate', as you seem to agree with me. In that moment you just stepped beyond belief into knowing what is 'truer' or more accurate for yourself. Information in the form of words pointed the way but you did the rest within your consciousness.

In a few moments I'm going to set up a comparison between believing and knowing. See how many times you nod your 'inner head' in agreement as you may or may not recognize the accuracy of the contrasts.

Remember I am not trying to convince you of anything. Simply sharing my personal perspective/perception through the medium of words so that it may help you do the same for your self.

Just as you cannot 'make' anyone believe anything, you cannot realize the truth, or 'greater accuracy', for someone else. We are each in the 'game of one', amongst the many. So never mind what anyone else believes or purports to know, including me. Only you can awaken your self to what you know is true or more accurate for you. But you can use the signposts that others offer you in many forms, from their words to the examples of their life.

These words are my offering to you.

As always I am available if anything is not clear
or if you have questions at
mike@relax7.com.

Part ONE

The difference between BELIEVING and KNOWING

Why do you pretend that you know
when you only believe?

What's the difference between
'the believer' and 'the knower'?

Why is it so often the case that
'those who know don't say
and those who say don't know'?

YOU are a Belief Creator

We are creators and sustainers of many different kinds of beliefs. For example, there are 'fatal beliefs'. Whenever you think or say, "I can't..." or "I am not able...", then it's highly likely you won't. There are 'blocker beliefs' that tend to be about other people. Whenever we judgmentally think or say, "She is an idiot or he is a stupid fool," often just throwaway comments in our cappuccino conversations, these beliefs block and distort the energy that you give to 'them' in the context of your relationship with them.

There are 'survival beliefs' to which most of us are exposed and then somewhat lazily assume are true, such as, "It's survival of the fittest" or "You have to look after number one" or "It's dog-eat-dog out there" or "The nature of the world is competitive". Holding these beliefs will guarantee you live your life in some form of fear.

Then there are 'flat earth' beliefs. These are beliefs that are obviously completely inaccurate. The physical evidence is so stacked against them yet people still 'believe'. For example, apparently there is a group of people in this world who believe that the earth is completely flat and that if you go over the edge you will find the dinosaurs on the other side! Say no more!

Having identified some of the categories of belief that we use to sabotage our self, many will say they believe there are also 'empowering beliefs'. Beliefs such as 'I believe I can' or 'I believe you are a good person' or 'I believe anything is possible'. However, I am going suggest that all beliefs are lies, that believing is a way of avoiding what is true, that belief is a sign of laziness, that all beliefs are traps that we don't realize we have created for our self, that all beliefs are guaranteed to cause the believer some form of suffering ...eventually.

Even those beliefs that 'seem' to empower!

Is it Possible?

It seems almost impossible not to believe in someone, something, some idea, some philosophy, some religious texts etc. You might be afraid not to have beliefs. Perhaps because you 'believe' you will be regarded as a vague, not all here, deluded, perhaps a bit of a 'wimp', if you don't have beliefs about something.

Belief, by definition, means you don't know. That's why belief must be accompanied by doubt. In truth doubt is not the opposite of belief. Doubt is your subconscious signaling you to be honest.

Subconsciously you know you don't know. Most of the time you are not consciously aware that believing is 'not knowing'. So belief will always have a cloud of doubt over it until you become consciously honest and say, "I believe it may be the true, but I don't really 'know' that to be true".

But most of the time many of us don't want to admit we don't really know. Especially when many others around us are claiming to know but are either unaware they don't or just won't admit they don't. Peer pressure seems to affect almost all of us.

We are quick to say, "My belief is....". But much less frequently do you hear people say, "But my doubt is..." That tends to be because belief is a fixed thing in the universe of consciousness. You can hang your hat on it! It seems to be a solid position. But doubt sits under and behind all beliefs like an amorphous cloud of greyness. You can't hold on to a cloud, but it's always there or it's always floating by.

Honest people, which usually means self-aware people, will usually express their doubts alongside their beliefs. They would say, "I believe that's how it works. I used to know, but I've forgotten. So I'm not so sure now".

"I used to know the way home like the back of my hand. But I've obviously forgotten. I believe it's this way. But I don't know for sure. Lets see!"

As doubt must exist when you believe, it means that unless you acknowledge your doubt and/or say, "I don't know", there will always be a tension, an anxiety, within your consciousness. It's this tension/anxiety that slowly but surely kills people. First it kills their enthusiasm, the vitality of their being. And some would say that's enough to define a life without liveliness. Eventually it may affect their physical health as the psychosomatic factor kicks in. There are already enough studies and books about that.

Three examples of why believing is not knowing.

1 Will your team win?

The football fan 'believes' his team is going to win this weekend. Why, because he wants to believe. He wants to be seen and heard as 'a believer'. Perhaps because he's learned to believe that 'believing' is a positive thing, a way to show support. But because the team has lost all of their last four games there will be a doubt that he is suppressing. Or deep down he knows he cannot feel as certain as the 'belief/thought' sounds.

All games are obviously unpredictable. Internally he is lost in the tension between his belief and his doubts. He may even believe that he has to believe in order to help the team, which means even more inner tension between belief and doubt. He may not notice but this tension will 'occupy' his thoughts and quietly diminish his vitality!

2 Are you really in love?

Then there's the young, newly married couple in which he believes she loves him. But there is always a doubt. Especially when behaviors often change after marriage. Or when actually living together reveals unexpected 'patterns'. The doubt must eventually surface as it makes its way from 'it's just a feeling' to thinking it and eventually into words and actions. This is why 'real love' is so rare in a relationship. It's why the word love is used so inaccurately to describe what is more often not love but dependency and neediness.

3 Are you a believer?

Then there is the religious believer. "I believe what I read in the 'good book'", says the religious enthusiast. In the first two examples you can get closer to 'knowing the truth' by being at the match to actually see what happens, or by asking your partner who is in front of you if they really do love you. But you cannot go back in time and verify anything in any scripture. You can never ever 'know' what is or is not true regarding any 'reporting' recorded in any scripture. It is, after all, just reporting and story telling.

Intuitively we all know this deep down. So there has to be very big doubts sitting behind any religious beliefs. There is likely to be a significant suppression of such doubts. For many it's not just suppression it's a matter of blanking out completely such doubt. Which is why you can't really have a 'two way conversation' for too long with many religious believers. They know that if they do you will likely end up at the question, "But how do you know?".

So they will try their best to avoid saying, "I don't know", with answers such as. "It's a matter of faith". They don't want to hear that faith is just 'belief without evidence'. If they do hear that, and acknowledge it, then their belief system, their support system, the personal identity that they have built out of their beliefs, will likely start to crumble. And that is not something they are willing to entertain ...generally speaking. Speak to any one who has had a 'crisis of faith' and they generally confirm they had long held but suppressed doubts. Along with a fear to say out loud, "I just don't know".

That's why spirituality is somewhat different from religion. The person walking an authentic spiritual path has realized that all false identities, especially those based on a belief system, have to collapse. They have to be 'seen through' in order to awaken to what is true and know that trueness for oneself.

They know that belief has nothing to say about truth. It may point but it can never capture. That's the purpose of this book. Only to point. Books cannot capture.

In reality our beliefs kill us. Not our body (immediately) but our 'self'. The moment we identify with them we kill our own authenticity. But we won't be aware of it. They kill our vitality as doubt drains our enthusiasm. We will distort our own energy into fear and anger whenever we perceive a threat or decide to defend the beliefs we are attached to. Any defensiveness is behavior based in fear. If the creation of such emotions that arise in defense of our beliefs become a habit they are likely to lead us down a path to the accelerated decay of our body. They will also send our intellect to sleep.

Beliefs are sleeping pills for our intellects. Just believing means we don't need to challenge, which means explore the accuracy of the belief. We allow them to shape our decisions and the direction of our life without question. From our beliefs come the thoughts and feelings that have an immediate affect on our wellbeing, and perhaps eventually, our physical health.

The Ideology of Belief

If we appear to others to be without belief in anything we often hear them say, "But you have to believe in something". But is not that in itself just another belief that is handed down and does the rounds as it spreads like a viral cliché from one mind to another?

Beliefs are viruses that take root and grow in our consciousness. If we are unaware of their presence they can cause many types of dis-ease within our consciousness, which 'may' eventually manifest as disease in our bodies. This is discussed in more detail in a previous book The Immune System of the Soul. Yes it can appear that the person motivated by and seemingly enthused by self-belief has 'high energy'. But such highs tend to be followed by lows. Ask anyone, driven by high self-belief, and they are likely to confirm that in quiet moments of self-reflection they also have significant self-doubt behind their apparent force of self-belief.

The most extreme form of the 'ideology of belief' can be seen in most religions today. If you are not a believer you are not only ostracized from the community of believers, your life may be violently ended. All because you do not profess to share the same 'beliefs' as those who do believe. Some say (believe) this is a form of insanity. Others say (believe) it's just human nature. And a few will say (believe) it's exactly how we remain asleep i.e. unaware of reality.

What do you see and say?

The Tyranny of Belief

So why exactly is belief so detrimental to our 'self'? What is the difference between believing and knowing exactly? Where does truth sit next to belief? And how do you free your self from the tyranny of the belief systems that you have, we all have, inherited and/or assimilated?

A belief is a fixed idea or concept about how the world 'is' and how it works. 'World' here can mean the world of your relationships, the physical world around you, the world of your thoughts and feelings, the world of your subconscious.

We create beliefs in our consciousness either from ideas/concepts that are handed to us through our upbringing, education or cultural influences. Or they can be formed entirely by ones self, within our consciousness, which is the self, usually during and after specific experiences. When we say 'my belief is...' in reference to our personally created beliefs, we are usually not aware that our creation has probably been heavily influenced by others beliefs sometime in the past. Sometimes it's called education.

So far so obvious. Beliefs in and off themselves are not bad or good, nor right or wrong. It's our relationship with our beliefs that cause us both a loss of vitality and some form of suffering. We tend to become attached to certain beliefs. All attachment must result in some form of anxiety (fear of loss) and therefore stress. Stressful relationships are simply the result of our beliefs being in contradiction to the other persons. That leads to the perception of others beliefs as a threat. This can be seen in almost every story on every page of every newspaper every day.

For example let's say you believe I 'have to' meet the deadline and I am entertaining the belief that I can't. But I believe that me meeting the deadline will make you happy. So I worry that I might make you unhappy if I miss the deadline because I still believe I am responsible for other people's happiness. So I believe I need to please others to 'get on' in life. Which means when someone is not pleased after something I have said or done, I believe it was me that made him or her unhappy.

But what if the truth is no one else is responsible for our happiness, that people please themselves, that whenever we become unhappy it's not the actions of another that makes us feel unhappy, it's our self. What if you 'know' that to be true for you? If you really 'knew' that, what difference would it make? In what ways would you think and act differently?

More people seem to be waking up to this kind of 'knowing what is truer' and realizing this is the basis of self-responsibility. But it has no power as long as its just words on this page and in your mind. It has to be fully realized within ones own consciousness if there is going to be a change of behavior and freedom from emotional suffering. This kind of truth is what's calling us to go and be beyond belief. Beyond our beliefs is a deeper awareness of what is true. The challenge is always bridging the gap between realizing our truth intellectually and bringing it through into new behaviors. From seeing to being to doing.

In this particular example it's seems to be much easier to keep believing that 'it's them' that makes me feel this way'. That's when an intellectual laziness sets in. We unknowingly sabotage our own consciousness. And before we know it our life becomes a journey in and out of the miseries of blaming and complaining, criticizing and resenting.

In the forthcoming pages my intention is not to try to tell you the truth. Although it may sometimes seem to sound like that. Please forgive me if it does. I am really just perceiving and thinking out loud as I dig deeper for myself.

The intention is to challenge the common beliefs I sense most of us have absorbed and lazily given the status of truth. In challenging I am pointing in other directions, highlighting what I perceive may be a greater 'accuracy', or a deeper dimension, around that topic.

Sometimes I will turn the whole belief system upside down. Frequently I will hesitate and challenge you with, "What do you think?" It's only by engaging with the ideas, concepts and insights within your own consciousness that you start to awaken what, for most of us, is our 'lazy intellect' and then 'see' for your self.   Then you are using the book and not just grazing the book. That way you get the most from the time you spend with the book.

Going a Little Deeper

As I now see it the root cause of all our miseries, all our moments of mental and emotional dis-ease, is when we create a belief and lose our sense of self in the belief. In other words our belief/s become the raw material out of which we construct a sense of identity - for anything from five seconds to five minutes to fifty years. This happens at a subtle level within our consciousness. So we don't notice it and no one teaches us how to notice it.

We learn this inner habit at a very young age, from parents and teachers. Then we teach it to the next generation. It seems it's pretty safe to say that everyone learns to make this mistake of creating their beliefs and then building a sense of identity out of their beliefs to some extent or other.

This creation of, attachment to, and identification with our beliefs ensures we remain closed and defensive, resistant and, for some of us, almost constantly on the offensive. The best time to notice this mistake of identifying with your beliefs is directly after an argument has ended.

If you reflect on the conversation you will notice you saw the other person's beliefs as a threat to you 'personally'. Simply because you were identifying your self with your belief. But you are not a belief. If you truly 'knew' this you would never be in conflict with anyone or anything. In response to this idea some people say, "I believe that would be incredibly boring". Which tends to indicate there is some form of emotional addiction. While others might say, "I now know that when I do not identify my self with any belief that's when I feel and know I am truly free".

Untangling Truth, Belief and Knowing

When you say I BELIEVE you are also saying I don't KNOW. If you knew you would not need to create and sustain the belief.

Don't know what? You don't know what is true or real for you. But it seems we don't want to be true to our self and say. "I don't know". That's why you will hear people speaking as if they know but they don't. They are simply sharing their belief. The moment they seek any kind of validation for their belief or they react to other people's beliefs that may contradict theirs, that's the moment you know they don't 'know'.

For example I could say I believe God exists. But that's like saying I don't know God exists. I don't say I believe the daffodils on my table are yellow. I know they are yellow. I can see them and touch them. So how do you know God exists? Only by meeting and seeing God directly. But if you met God would you meet an individual being with a personality or an impersonal entity or an omnipresent energy. How would you know that you met and were in the presence of God? Or would you just create the belief that you just met God? Perhaps because someone whispered over your shoulder their belief, "That's God".

Some will say that it's through 'feeling the presence' of such a being that they now know such a being exists. But could that also just be another belief based on a personal interpretation of a feeling. It sometimes suits us to interpret our feelings as the fulfillment of our desires. Especially if it also marks us out as someone special, one of the few who has met and now knows God.

As you can see, separating believing and knowing is tricky.

Back to our questions. Questioning is something we don't often do when we have decided on what we believe. Believers don't seem to question, doubt, explore and inquire ...so much. They are not so curious. Why should they be, when they already have well-formed and fixed beliefs, often masquerading as 'I know...'. Curiosity would then be an admission of not knowing. Honesty might prevail. But our old friend the ego doesn't like that.

What are the signs of the difference between someone who has created and is holding a belief and someone who has realized and knows that belief is not the truth? How do you know you don't know? How often do you say 'I know' when you really just believe? Why can't we just say, 'I don't know?'

These are all challenging questions in the process of untangling belief, knowing and truth. If we don't untangle and clarify there is a good chance we will allow what we believe, but don't know, to misguide our entire life. What do you think? Is that true for you? Is that idea pointing at the reality of how many of us live our life?

The Ultimate Humility

When it comes to the practical things in life, things that require action, it's not difficult to say without ego or arrogance, "I know how to do that" or "I don't know how to do that". But when it comes to the less tangible and the 'what's happening in your consciousness' aspects of life, it's not so easy.

It requires a certain humility to say, "I don't know". Especially if we have been brought up in a culture that feeds you approval and acceptance when you 'appear' to demonstrate that you know. Most education systems are based on testing your knowledge and rewarding you for it. But is it true knowledge? Do you truly know, or is it simply your ability to memorize information that is tested? Are you rewarded for knowing or memorizing? Is remembering the information, the theory, enough to say that you 'know'?

Yes, perhaps it is, with regard to the mathematical, mechanical, technological aspects of life. Memorizing the formula is said to be enough to say you know. But do you really know until you've used it or applied it? Then you know for sure!

With regard to aspects of your self, your consciousness, the YOU, what do you know? Most people, if they were honest, would probably say, "I don't know my self very well". Others might say, "I don't know myself at all". And perhaps some would say, with the ultimate humility, "I know that I just don't know me"!

So, with that in mind, lets continue with a comparison between believing and knowing. See what rings bells for you and where you might locate your self on the continuum between the two ends of the spectrum, between believing and knowing, including knowing when you don't know!

1 STATIC and FLUID

The believer tends to be STATIC whereas the knower, who knows they don't know, tends to be FLUID. The believer tends to have a fixed and narrow mindset defined by their belief. They become stuck and static around their belief. Whereas the 'don't knower' and the knower tend to be malleable and fluid.

They have realized that knowing has many levels and depths that have yet to be realized. They are prepared to release what they know now and welcome a deeper current of 'knowingness' to flow into their awareness.

Practical Example: The believer has settled on one way to cook rice. As far as they are concerned they believe their way is the 'only best' ...way! The knower will say there are probably many ways to cook rice. They know they don't know them all and they are ready to hear and learn and thereby 'come to know' more.

2 CLOSED and OPEN

The believer tends to be CLOSED around their beliefs/s. Within their consciousness it's as if they wrap themselves in their belief system, which becomes a comfort blanket.   They will cry if it's taken away. They will be constantly anxious that someone will remove it, that someone else's beliefs may seem to be truer or more accurate.

Whereas the knower who knows they don't know is not only OPEN and ready to welcome others beliefs and ideas, they are curious and enquiring.   Their openness allows them to expand and deepen their awareness.

Practical Example: The believer will say this particular way home is always the fastest way home from here. The knower knows that there are many ways home and the quickness varies from day to day depending on circumstances such as traffic. They know they don't know the fastest way on that day, but they are open to finding it.

3 ATTACHED and NON-ATTACHED

The believer tends to become ATTACHED to their beliefs to the extent that they will find themselves unknowingly using their beliefs to create their sense of identity. Religious people (not all) tend to do this with ease. They take the information from their scriptures and form their own version of the beliefs and then create the belief that 'I am a Christian' or 'I am a Hindu' or 'I am a Moslem' etc.

They create a religious identity. They identify themselves with an idea, with a belief. They have not yet realized that the self, the conscious being, the 'I' that says 'I am', is not an idea, not a belief. The self creates beliefs. The creator is not the creation. But it's hard for a 'religious believer' to hear that, never mind contemplate it's accuracy.

Whereas the knower who knows they do not know doesn't become attached to any idea, concept or belief.   They know that they are not a belief or belief system. They know that to create an identity out of anything that is not ones self, such as ideas or beliefs, and even the experiences of others, (scriptural records) is to create an ego i.e. an illusion about who I am.   They know the ego then causes the self to create conflict with others and thereby suffer in different ways.

4 DEFENSIVE and EMBRACING

Believers tend to become DEFENSIVE and/or aggressive (which is also a form of defensiveness), when they perceive their beliefs are being challenged and therefore threatened. They mistakenly believe their beliefs are 'the truth' and they believe 'I have the truth' and you don't. This sits at the heart of all religious conflict and indeed any argument that occurs in any context.

The knower never holds any belief to be true. The knower has realized and knows that 'truth' is a personal state of being which is unique to each one of us, and can never be captured in words or any kind of physical symbol.

They know that the truth is not a thing or a concept. The knower knows that truth does not need to be defended or protected. But the believer tends to be frequently defensive; unaware they are making themselves suffer in such moments.

For example, almost all resistance movements in society in general, and in the arenas of politics and the environment in particular, are based on groups of people who believe they know the truth! They believe they have to fight those whom they believe don't know the truth, in order to re-establish the truth. Hence the emergence of resistance and protest movements.

Instead of dialogue, relationship building and mutual exploration, one side tries to force their 'beliefs' on others. The result? Division and two conflicted and unhappy groups of believers under the illusion 'we know better' without realizing it really means 'we believe better'.

Have you ever heard someone say, "I believe better than you?"

5 IDEALISED and REALISED

The believer tends to be 'IDEALISTIC'. At the core of their beliefs are ideas about how they think things 'should be' in their world, and how other people 'should be' in their world ...ideally. They may spend much time and energy on trying to make their ideals real and as a result frequently making themselves disappointed and angry. Many point to this process to explain the 'evolution of the cynic'. Sometimes defined as a disappointed idealist.

The knower is a 'REALIST' and has recognized that all ideas and concepts are just that, ideas and concepts. They are not the basis of 'reality', which is ever changing. They can never be imposed. The knower knows everything just is what it is, as it is, at any given moment.

They have realized that everything and everyone is exactly the way they are meant to be, at any given moment. They tend therefore to live more in the reality of the moment. To try to impose a set of ideals, which is just a set of beliefs, upon others would be both arrogant and futile in the mind of the knower who knows they don't know.

6 VALIDATION and DEEPER INSIGHT

The believer tends to seek consciously and subconsciously for confirmation and VALIDATION of their beliefs, often mistaking it for validation of ones self. Hence the believer tends to feel insecure to some extent or another.

The knower never seeks validation for any belief. They know what they know, and they know there is always more to know, and they are likely to know what they do not yet know! For the knower the process of knowing what is true and real is never-ending and depthless.

They are continuously inquiring and exploring the depths of their own consciousness. They don't need to seek validation or any kind of confirmation as they are never fixed in their viewpoint or understanding.

7 NOT SO HONESTY and OPENLY HONEST

The believer tends to suffer from frequent periods of unhappiness simply because they are not being honest. They are using belief to suppress doubt. They are subjecting themselves to an inner anxiety. They are saying 'I Know', when they really only believe. They can't bring themselves to say 'I don't know'. Or they are just not aware they don't know.

Someone who knows they don't know is truer to themselves on the inside. They know they don't know everything. They never build the facade of knowing in order to disguise the doubt that must accompany belief. They are not suppressing anything as they are deeply curious and interested in when they may realize the next level, the deeper truth, the new insight, and what that insight may be.

8 EMOTIONAL REACTION and COOL RESPONSE

The believer will be frequently emotional as they are attached to their beliefs. Attachment to any idea, concept, memory or belief guarantees the creation of emotions such as fear or sadness or anger. Fear of loss when their belief maybe exposed as false. Sadness when loss is perceived i.e. when someone demonstrates greater clarity around what they believe. And anger towards the perpetrator/event that apparently exposed their belief to be just that, a belief that is not true or accurate.

The knower seldom becomes emotional as they have ended their attachment to all ideas, concepts and beliefs. They know that's it's unhealthy to hold on to any fixed position. Internally they are no longer 'trapped in' any belief or belief system. They are internally free.

This allows them to 'feel' and apply their intuitive wisdom from inside out without the noise of emotion getting in the way. They are humbly receptive to all other points of view. This, in turn, empowers them in the process of creating the clearest, wisest and the most appropriate response to situations and people in their life.

9 FALSE CERTAINTY and AUTHENTIC DOUBT

The believer often has a forced attitude of CERTAINTY, which also disguises the suppression of their doubts. The knower who knows they don't know allows their doubts to arise into the clear light of their consciousness as they inquire and explore within themselves the deeper dimensions of what 'may be' truer or more real.

Their uncertainty is consciously created so that they may remain open to see and know with greater clarity. Paradoxically this strengthens their ability to access that deeper wisdom within themselves whenever they have to make challenging decisions or offer others advice.

10 MEMORY to MIND and INTUITION to INTELLECT

Beliefs are held firmly in memory. They shape perception and generate thoughts, which show up in the mind. As long as you are operating from belief you will not be able to fully 'feel intuitively' and hear your intuitive wisdom. Does that sound right to you? Please don't believe it. Go into it and see if you can see for your self. The words are just signposts remember?

This is why most of us live reactive lives. We allow the 'beliefs program' we received from others and installed in our own consciousness to generate our reactions to other people and to life itself. Whereas, when we free our self from all beliefs, from the whole program, we can then start to respond from our heart. Not from emotion. Emotion does not come from the heart of you. It comes as a result of your attachment to something or someone in your mind. Can you see this?

The knower knows this so they deliberately take time out to meditate, to contemplate, which is another way of saying going beyond the beliefs they hold in memory. They go to a deeper place within themselves, to the heart of their being, (not their body) where they feel and hear the 'subtle voice of the heart' itself. This is the voice that awakens and empowers their intellect.

11 TALKS and SILENT

The believer tends to talk a lot about their beliefs! Often driven by a subconscious urge to prove their beliefs are true. They want others to believe they know. They are attempting to impose their beliefs on others out of the need to dominate, and then to garner the support of others so they can say, "Look, see, he's with me on this. What I say must be true because they agree".

The knower says little. They know that as soon as you start to speak you are trying to do the impossible, which is capture the truth in words. Hence that old saying 'those who say don't know while those who know don't say'.

12 BLIND FAITH and ENLIGHTENED FAITH

The believer and the knower may both have 'faith' but their sources of faith are different. The believer's faith is forcefully based on 'belief with no evidence'. Likely absorbed from some external source like a book or a group philosophy. The believer will say their evidence comes from outside in, from the words and beliefs of others.

The knower's faith comes from inside out. It arises from a trust in ones intuitive feelings. These feelings are subtle but when 'listened to' the knower is able to realize for themselves what is truer. They notice that their 'knowingness' refines itself over time. It's never fixed. They are good listeners always open to hear others as well as their own inner voice in response to others.

They are continuously cultivating their awareness, always consulting their own intuition. They know they are in a process of progressive enlightenment.

The more this occurs and the deeper it occurs the greater their faith that their enlightenment is real and happening. Eventually faith itself becomes redundant.

Replaced by a 'quiet knowingness'.

13 LIMITED and UNLIMITED

We often hear and read about the possibility of getting rid of your limiting beliefs. Seminars, workshops and books are frequently positioned with such a promise. But the knower knows that, by definition, ALL beliefs are limiting. Simply because they are static, fixed, closed ideas, made into 'things' and held firmly within and by consciousness. To such an extent that consciousness itself becomes 'lost in' and 'defined by' such ideas/concepts etc.

The knower has realized that when consciousness itself is in its most natural state it is fluid, open, flexible, and free of all attachment to any thing/idea/concept. This also describes the unlimited nature of the self.

As the mystics have reminded us it seems this unlimited and unbounded state of being is an intrinsic, already present, characteristic of consciousness. It's the limiting nature of any and ALL beliefs that gets in the way of being aware of and knowing our true nature as unlimited beings.

Beliefs in and of themselves are limitations. They are what we use to limit our self. Hence the awareness of 'being beyond belief' is where the knower knows the reality of their own unlimitedness.

Would you agree?

If not, why not?

If so, why so?

If your perceptions and thoughts are not so clear why not take a piece of paper and write a paragraph with your personal 'take' on believing and knowing.

You will likely find that when you listen to your self in this way you will start to realize what you know but didn't know you knew.

Part TWO

Journeys
BEYOND BELIEF

Exploring the 7 Deadly Beliefs

At the end of the last book, The Journey from IGNORANCE to ENLIGHTENMENT, I briefly listed what I called the 'seven deadly beliefs'. Here they are in all their glory with a challenge to see, go and be beyond each one.

RESPONSIBILITY

BEYOND BELIEF

How do you feel?
Upset you say
When I spoke those words
The other day

You pointed at me
With thought and finger
You accused, you blamed
With a look that lingered

For just a moment
If a glance could kill
I'd be horizontal
At your darkest will

It's you, not me
You still believe
It's the others fault
You still perceive

But the day it dawns
That it's never the other
Is the day you're free
From blaming another

All your hurts
Are self-inflictions
Your thoughts and emotions
Your own creations

It's not what they said
That makes you feel this way
It's what you do
With what they do or say

So take back your power
Be a victim no more
If you can say 'it's me'
You won't make your self sore

You have been brilliantly taught to believe other people and the world are responsible for what you feel and how your life unfolds.

Just not true!

When you believe that other people are responsible for your feelings you will develop the habits of resentment and perhaps hatred when they don't be or do what you want or expect.

When you believe events in the world are responsible for what you feel you will develop anxiety and worry as you consume the news.

When you believe your circumstances are defined by what you own you will develop the habits of insecurity and unhappiness.

Put them all together and you will see and believe your self to be a victim, as someone who is not responsible for themselves or their circumstances.

You will be frequently visited by feelings of powerlessness and inadequacy. You will likely waste time and energy going over who and what and why others are to blame for your feelings and your life. This will drain your energy and eventually the habit of apathy will replace any enthusiasm you may have had. Your beliefs are killing you! But you probably won't notice.

You may attend many seminars, listen to many gurus of personal growth, read many books, and experiment with many techniques to get your life on your chosen track. But until you kill this one belief nothing will work for more than a short period.

The truth is you are entirely responsible for your every thought, feeling and behavior. At all times. Why, because you create them! There is no one else in your head doing it for you. It's as simple as that.

Would you agree?

But then you may ask, "What about my parents, or my teachers or my childhood or my nasty brother or the violent culture of this society - surely they have been responsible for some of the things I think and feel?"

Nice try! The full realization that you are entirely responsible in this moment now can only occur when you notice that the world and people out there are, in reality, 'in here'! You create within your consciousness your version of the world 'out there'. But we each create differently. If we didn't we would be clones.

As a child you did not know this. As a teenager you did not know this. As an adult you probably still do not know this. No one has been able to illustrate why this is so, simply because so few people know and even fewer are able live it.

But now you are coming to know. The theory at least! The next step is to see the truth of this for your self. If you don't then nothing is going to fundamentally shift within your consciousness, within you. And it's likely nothing significant will change lastingly for the better in your life.

Why do people see the same events but have radically different responses? Why do you really like a person yet some of your friends hate that same person? Why do you look forward to going home at Christmas or Diwali or whenever, and yet your brother or sister, dread it? Why can you laugh when your best friend mocks you but hate it when a colleague at work does the same?

Isn't it obvious? At every moment we are each creating the world and our relationships in our own unique way. The world seems to be 'out there' but you are constantly creating your personal version of everything and everyone 'in here'!

When you awaken to this reality you will start to re-empower your self. You will stop giving your power away. You will start to wonder why you create some things darkly and other things brightly! But most of all you will see that when there is darkness, when you feel dark and think dark things, that you are the creator of any and all darkness around anything and everything.

This realization is tremendously freeing. Some people hate it as it means their thoughts and feelings arising from the 'I am a victim' belief are no longer true and will have to come to an end. They have become comfortable being a victim.

Others embrace this insight as it means they get their life back. They can stop seeing themselves as the victim and start creating their life consciously.

What about you?

Does this make sense to you?

Take a moment. Stare at the ceiling. Recall three times in the last few days when you projected your unhappiness onto someone else or something else.

Can you see, do you now know, it wasn't them, it was you?

First the theory, then the practice.

HAPPINESS

BEYOND BELIEF

You search high and low
For the holy grail
Going here and there
Just ensures you fail

You try this and that
Hoping you'll find
The deepest contentment
For your busy mind

Some are waiting forever
For happiness eventually
They don't want to hear
It's up to you, essentially

Many look back
To a happier past
Hoping for a return
And that it will last

But it's here, not there
It's now, not then
It's been with you forever
Until who knows when

Just learn to be quiet
Then see and feel
It's what you are
When you're being real

Just say it and feel it
"I am happy now"
Just show it and give it
Then take a bow

**If you have learned to believe that happiness is found
'out there' in the world you are guaranteed
to make your self unhappy.**

Unfortunate but true!

'How to be happy' is one of the most popular questions on Quora. Unfortunately it's probably not the best question regarding happiness. Better to ask, "Why am I not happy now'?

Only when you start to ask that question do you become curious. That curiosity will invite you to look at what you are doing within your consciousness that is making you unhappy. It also means you have started to stop searching for what you can never find.

Introspective curiosity is the sign you have begun your journey back to your personal version of happiness. 'Journey back' means you were once naturally happy. It's still your nature to be happy. Most authentic spiritual paths remind us it's a core state of being that is always accessible. But we learn to keep sabotaging it.

Almost all the beliefs in this book will be what you are unconsciously using to make your self an unhappy camper ...as they say. But you are seldom aware of it.

Your 'personal version' of happiness means you can't have anyone else's happiness. You can never know anyone else's happiness. Unfortunately one of the most common methods to sabotage your happiness is with the belief that you should be and could be as happy as 'them'. From that comes the perpetual desire to acquire what others seem to have that is 'apparently' making them happy. Not to mention 'continuous comparisons' with others and the futile attempt to measure your happiness against theirs.

Asking 'why am I not happy' initiates introversion. An inner enquiry commences. You will then start to notice specific emotions of unhappiness such as sadness, anger and fear. These are the three universal signs that you have lost your ability to be in your most natural state, which is the deepest happiness i.e. contentment. But fortunately it's only ever a temporary loss.

So lets cut to the chase. There is a slew of beliefs about happiness that you have likely absorbed and assimilated that are polluting your consciousness and disconnecting you from your true underlying contented nature. They are obvious in theory but hard to shake off in reality. Especially when everyone around you has also been hypnotized by the same beliefs. Such as:

1   Happiness 'only' comes with success in the world, the achievement of ones goals in the world, getting what you want from the world.

2   It's what other people do or say that makes you happy (see Responsibility).

3   Happiness only comes from outside in, through some kind of stimulation.

4   Happiness is what happens when you are recognized by others in some way.

As long as your moments of unhappiness are still tolerable you will not enquire as to why you are unhappy so frequently. You won't see the belief you are carrying about happiness that is making you unhappy. You will keep believing in and seeking the drugs of stimulation, recognition, approval, acceptance, acquisition and achievement. They will continue to alleviate your small and even major miseries. Until they don't.

But if you are interested in the truth about happiness and you would like to rediscover the reality of that truth within your self, you will one day say, enough is enough!

You will sit down and enquire either in your self, or perhaps through some books, or the wisdom of the wiser, as to 'why am I not happy so often'. When the penny drops and you realize the world, which includes other people, are not designed to make you happy you are on the way. Then you 'know' it's all down to you. It's your job. It's an inside job.

If you sustain your curiosity you will gradually notice how ALL the beliefs that you're carrying within your consciousness are the cause of your discontentment.

Start now. Stop reading, take a walk, stare out the window, contemplate the flames in the fire, with one question in mind. Why am I not happy now?

If you say to your self, "I don't know" stay in your 'don't know mindset', then start to become fully aware of the exact nature of your unhappiness. Whatever form or feeling it seems to take. Make this your mission.

If you look your unhappiness in the eye, so to speak, without resistance or judgment, without desire for relief, you will notice that's when it starts to subside.

Why are you unhappy? You already know. Start writing it down. What are YOU putting in the way? Not who is getting in the way! What within you are you doing that is killing your happiness?

What is happiness, exactly?

Ask your friends and begin a conversation. Only a few will want to be introspective and reflective with you. Hang out with those friends. Journey together.

It's almost the only journey truly worthy of your footsteps.

SUCCESS

BEYOND BELIEF

The chase is on
You're in the race
As you pursue
Fame for your face!

Applause and approval
Your daily measures
When you believe
They're your rightful treasures

Your incessant longing
To celebrate
Ensures you live
By anxieties gate

But success is not
What you achieve
That's what you're taught
To blindly believe

Success is not
Just crossing the line
Wearing your medals
For the rest of your time

The day will come
You will have to discern
What is success for me
Beyond what I earn

Is it just to be happy?
Or is it much deeper
To love and be loved
Or to be your own keeper

Ask a thousand people
What is success for you?
All with different beliefs
In this moment all true

You have probably assimilated the belief that success has something to do with accumulation and/or achievement.

Is that true, for you?

What does success mean to you? Is it the achievement of a lifelong ambition, a goal that has required steely determination, the completion of a minor task, the finding of the perfect partner, the making of a million, the trophy at the end of the tournament, surviving the greatest storm.

Defining success is always a personal choice. Many of us will, one day, find a quiet room or an empty field or a mountaintop or the serenity of a flat calm lake, and then contemplate and ruminate on one of the biggest questions in life, 'what is success for me'.

Whatever you decide, discern, intuit or settle for, even then it's likely to change according to your age, circumstances and relationships. So you will need to review it and renew it frequently. Or perhaps revise it completely.

Many, if not most of us, will not ruminate or review. We will opt for the easy way, the lazy road, as we absorb and live out other people's definitions of success. Watching sport is a popular way to live vicariously through the public success of others. We identify with their feats and achievements and then celebrate them as if they were our own.

Envying the wealth of others, admiring the appearance of others, talking about the achievements of others, are all ways in which we live through others apparent success. But they are just ways of avoiding the question 'what does success mean to me'?

As an experiment, imagine the following were the parameters of success you were taught as a child. Imagine you can see numerous examples around you every day. Which one appeals to you most?

Success is:

- Acting with total honesty and integrity thus generating a clear conscience (without which the authentic happiness that we call 'contentment' is impossible)

- Remaining peaceful and stable when all around you are in crisis or chaos

- Valuing what you 'are' more than what you have (but then what are you?)

- Being able to see past the weaknesses/mistakes of others and focus on their inherent goodness/strengths

- Being able to let go of the past and thereby not allowing it to cloud your judgment in the present

- Giving without the desire for anything in return

Perhaps one stands out. Perhaps they all seem to have merit. Perhaps you have your own parameters for success. You will obviously be the one to decide. When you do you will know to what extent it is shaping your life by how much it consciously informs your decisions and by the way you relate to others.

Like happiness, success is defined in many ways, at many levels by many people. It's so easy to absorb their beliefs and then try to make them our own. Imitation follows. Comparisons follow. Until you realize your journey, your destination is entirely in your hands.

Find a tree. Sit quietly. Reflect deeply. Enquire curiously. Decide slowly. Ask your self, "In which context or area of my life should I define success first". Then ask, "What are all the areas/contexts in my life in which I could define success"?

What would constitute success in each context?

Then perhaps ask your self, "In my life as a whole what might success look like"?

Try not to create more beliefs about success. Once you have a little clarity and a few ideas, let them all go and get on with living. If your reflections and realizations were authentic they will naturally inform your decisions and direction. Sometimes without you being consciously aware that they do so.

If they weren't authentic, they wont.

Sound like hard work?

Building the foundation has to take a little effort and attention. Otherwise the building is shaky and vulnerable.

Besides, it's not work, it's an adventure!

IDENTITY

BEYOND BELIEF

Something long forgotten
May dawn on you today
A mystery revealed
Brings wisdom of the way

The way to be, the way to live
The way to feel and think and see
To create, and then to give
From knowing 'I am free'

Free to be your self again
A liberation from illusion
The stripping of all labels
The dissolving of delusion

Who you think you are
Is not what you believe
It's not what you've been taught
But it's really hard to see

It's the paradox of 'self'
No thing, no one, no body
Just the 'I' that says 'I am'
Simply being ...nobody!

One day you'll have this clarity
About who and what you are
It's a moment drawing closer
The most beautiful by far

It's in the mirror of the other
You will know your self as 'me'
Without any further labels
At last you will be free

Just watch what you're doing
Prior to your thoughts and feelings
Know from where they come
And realize your self as 'being'

**The most frequent mistake you have learned to make,
hundreds of times every day, is to believe
you are someone you're not!**

But then, who are you, in truth?

At the level of personal identity your consciousness is similar to the consciousness of almost every human being. It is filled with a thousand beliefs about 'who I am' that are not true!

If only you knew! Only a very few seem to know. Probably a fraction of a percent of the entire population of planet earth seems to know! Although many will say they know 'who I am', in reality it's unlikely. It seems more likely they 'believe' they know. But, as we explored in part one, believing is not knowing. Their behavior is the giveaway. When you 'know' who you are, what you are, unhappiness is impossible. Hate and resentment are impossible. Fear and sorrow are impossible. Impatience and blame are impossible, when you know your self as you are, as the 'I' that says 'I am'.

Ignorance of this one aspect of all our lives sits at the root cause of all our conflicts both between us and within us. The three emotions of almost perpetual unhappiness - sadness, anger and fear - arise with daily regularity out of this one ignorance of 'who am I'.

If only you knew! You would never be unhappy again, never be unloving again, never be discontent again.

But we like our ignorance. At least, in our ignorance, we believe we do! Ignorance is bliss, they say. But that's probably a million miles from the truth. In the question of 'who am I' ignorance is suffering.

The realization of the 'truth of you' starts with 'seeing' and realizing who you are not. Stripping your self naked of all the things you are using to build your sense of identity, your many identities, every day. Then, when all the labels, beliefs, ideas about your self are gone, seeing what is left. Being what remains. That'll be you. Unfortunately most people won't do that simply because it's like asking someone to take off all their clothes and walk down the street naked. It's not going to happen, for most.

Besides there seems to be some kind of perverted comfort in trying to be someone we are not. In being the parent, in being the manager, in being the owner of that shiny car, in being a member of that national clan, or that cult, or that particular philosophy, or that race, or those beliefs, or this particular gender. They are all manufactured identities that are not the authentic self.

There is no conspiracy to keep you deluded as to who 'you really are'. There is no one trying to keep you in the dark. It's just a trap that everyone is led into by those who are unwittingly already there!

The fleeting comfort that each one of the above can momentarily bring you, as the car impresses, the parent is obeyed, the manager is followed, the philosophy and beliefs are lauded, the race stand together, is always and only ever temporary. They are the comforts of the ego. Yes the ego is another word for ignorance. It is the deepest ignorance, if ignorance could be described as 'deep'. It is this false belief about 'who I am' that now inhabits the world within the consciousness of almost every human being like a virus.

Between moments of temporary relief and comfort we lapse back into sorrow and neediness, into stress and dependency, into emotional suffering and eventually despair. Are you there? Do you have such insperiences? They are tolerable until they're not! Are you ready to strip? You may not be ready. Not everyone is ready. Few are really ready to return to being a 'naked being'.

If you think you are, I dare you to strip. In the safety of your own consciousness of course. In the changing room of your own mind. Strip away all the things that you use to try to be 'someone' in the story of your life. Ask your self what am I attached to. The answer will give you clues as to what you are using to clothe your self, clothe your consciousness. Then you can experiment with taking those clothes off.

See how it feels. Watch your self want to rebel. Be aware of your own resistance to realizing what you are using to create a fictional you.

You will eventually encounter the flimsiest clothing made of the beliefs that you have created, sustained and carried during your life so far. Your beliefs are just veils that you wear and hide behind. It doesn't matter what the content of the belief is. It doesn't matter how true you believe your belief is. It's just another veil. Keep unveiling your self and your 'authenticity' will eventually shine out and into the world anew.

Gradually, as you peel everything away, you will come to realize who you really are, which is nothing more or less than awareness itself. Pure awareness. Undressed consciousness. Vacant emptiness. Finally, the beliefless being that is you. All of which is a description of no one, as in nobody.

Yes it may sound daft. It may trigger within you a perception of a threat, a feeling of huge insecurity, even a kind of futility. But if you stay with it. If you go into nakedness. If you continue to be naked. It will be like you did take off all your physical clothes and did walk down the high street, naked in public. And you realized after ten minutes how freeing it is. How real it is. How natural it is. How unselfconscious you could be while being looked at by others. Ask anyone who has done it and many will tell you a tale of liberation and exhilaration.

But this is not about naked bodies. This is about naked being. To be naked is to be no one. Then you are free. Authentic. Natural. Liberated. Just being your self. At last!

Now life doesn't stop there. It just begins. As you carry that awareness into all that you do you start to 'play' at life as opposed to being played by life. You can start to be extremely creative in the many roles that you play. Because now you know you are not the role but the creator and the player of each and every role. Now you don't build an identity out of titles. You play with the title, quietly knowing this is not me.

If you can maintain this awareness life will become creative and playful, open and fluid, humble and yet a powerful example for others.

However, because of all the other beliefs that are installed within your consciousness you will frequently lose this awareness of 'who I really am', of being naked. So you will need to keep restoring it.

As a child you probably fell off your bike a lot when you were learning to ride. Until one day you mastered it. It's exactly the same. You will lose this awareness of who you are and drop back into trying to 'be someone' until you have mastered being no one, which is the same as being your self.

The outcome is similar to mastering that bike. A new freedom is discovered. There's a liberation from the old and familiar. Just as you rode your bike through the woods with the wind in your hair and new joy sprung into your heart, you start to ride through your life and the winds of adversity become gentle breezes at your back.

But you won't know it by just believing it.

Take a pen and a blank page and write down ALL that YOU are not.

Keep writing until there is nothing left to write.

Then ask your self 'who is writing'?

SECURITY

BEYOND BELIEF

If money could talk
What might it say?
Put me down
Put me away

Why do you count me?
Why do you say
If you had more of me
Then you'd be OK

I am not your savior
Not even your rock
I can't change your feelings
That's your job, don't stop

I'm here only to help
With clothing and food
Not to bring you success
Or make you look good

So use me not abuse me
As we spend time together
I'm just here to help
Whatever the weather

Don't make me your enemy
I can be your best friend
But just when together
We share benevolent ends

I'm not all for you
So give me away
To those who are needy
And have nothing today

You'll know when you do
There's a feeling so true
When sharing your pennies
Enriches you

**Every day you absorb the myth that your sense
of security is dependent on that
'material stuff' called money.**

Of course you already know, it isn't!

When you make your sense of security dependent on money or any of the material stuff of life you are guaranteed to make your self feel insecure. This paradox haunts most of our lives. It's one of the first 'bits' of belief programming we receive from parents, teachers and society at large. It's all around us every day.

Most of us will spend our entire lives in various states of anxiety never knowing the real meaning or feeling of security. We may read all the get rich quick books and buy into the philosophies of all the preachers of 'money making made easy', but still we will be anxious.

Even if we do make a million we will still worry. We will probably still be nervously concerned. Even the wealthy still envisage a life of poverty and debt. In fact it's now fairly well recognized that, for many, the more money they have the more insecure they will be.

Yes there are people who are relaxed and easy in their relationship with money. But it's also likely they would be the same if they had almost none.

So what's the solution to insecurity that arises from financial aspirations? How are we to live in such a way so that whether money comes or goes we are unperturbed and undisturbed?

It requires the transfer of our perceived source of security from outside to inside. Outside is the paymaster, the banks, the government, the stock markets, the house price, the salary. Over which you have absolutely no control. As the adverts tell us everything rises and falls in material value. Everything comes and goes in the material river of life.

Step one is to accept this and stop trying to hold back the tides in your head with something called worry. Notice you are misusing your imagination. Find more productive ways to exercise your mental creativity.

Step two is to contemplate the real and deeper meaning of 'security'. Notice, when you feel secure within your self, what are you feeling? Babies feel secure when they are feeling loved. But not for long, as love from others, like money, starts to come and go as they grow.

Notice how you feel most secure when you are giving your love as care, as help, as guidance, as compassion. Over this you do have control. These are moments when you 'know your value' as a human being. You don't need to think it, be told it, be given it, or receive it. It's not an intellectual insight. It's just a feeling that tells you that you just know your own value.

Along with this feeling comes an 'intuitive knowingness' that, at this level, your value can never be taken from you. But you also know that in order to sustain this state of knowingness, this state of feeling secure in your self, all your habits of neediness and the dependency have to come to an end. The fastest way to do that is to replace them with your generosity and kindness of spirit.

So this is the challenge almost all of us face. How to make our self of value to others in the currency exchange called relationship AND non-dependent on the returns. One way is investment. If you invest your money carefully you will receive, in time, a handsome return. Money is just a symbol for energy. So where could you invest your energy, the energy of you, your consciousness, which would give you a good return. Not a return from others but a return that shows up as the formless feelings of your own heart.

To receive an answer to this question from within your self you will need to free your self from the belief in entitlement. You have no right to security, monetary or otherwise. It's something you have to create for your self. Can you see this? It's tough, especially if you have been brought up in a rights based society that teaches an entitlement mindset.

The beliefs that "I deserve, I have a right, I am owed, I am entitled' are all programmed in. But they just make you lazy. If you challenge them you will eventually realize they are just not true. It's not how life works. They are only valid in the context of protecting the vulnerable. It's just that more and more people have started to 'choose to believe' that not only are they vulnerable but being this kind of vulnerable is the best way to live a lazy life.

Your sense of security will arise naturally when you invest your time and energy wisely in the context of your relationships. Ask anyone who cares for others, who serves others, without wanting return and they will tell you how the feeling of insecurity, which is just another form of fear, subsides. They don't start thinking, "Oh now I am secure". The feelings of insecurity in the forms of anxiety and worry simply fade.

How do you know? You don't know, until you take that risk to invest your energy wisely, lovingly, carefully, benevolently. You don't know, until you start to give your 'self' away.

But what does it really mean to you 'to invest ones energy wisely' in the real time context of your life? What does time and energy spent wisely look like to you?

May you reflect brightly and contemplate deeply these questions for your self. When you do you may be surprised by your own wisdom.

If you're not, drop me a line!

LOSS

BEYOND BELIEF

Trained to see
What's gone from me
We sit and fret
About what's going next

It's all because
We invented 'mine'
We forget all things
Must go in time

But when you realize
No thing belongs to me
No one is ever mine
At last you can be free

Then it's easy to release
What you used to hold
It's easy to let go
And allow your life to flow

Then the magic happens
All things will come to thee
If you can just be open
All things will come to be

That's why they often say
Be careful what you wish
Eventually it will happen
But it won't restore your bliss

It's hardest with another
You want them to 'be mine'
But they cannot be possessed
Just briefly present for this time

So release all that you have
From the grasp of mind and heart
Allow all things to come and go
Each day a fresh new start

**Perhaps the greatest and deepest belief
is the (be) <u>lie</u> (f) that you have
something to lose!**

But you 'know' you don't, don't you?

Why are so many of us miserable with such regularity? Why is depression a global phenomenon? Depression is projected to become the biggest killer on the planet by 2020 according to the World Health Organization. Could it be down to one belief? One belief, that lives in the consciousness of almost every human being in every culture. A belief that must cause some form of sadness, the precursor to depression.

The belief in 'possession'. We all grow up believing we can and should aspire to possess. It doesn't matter what it is. Just make sure you get what you want. And if you don't get what you want, get what you can. If you can't get it easily, take it, grab it. Make it yours. Be in possession! If you do we will celebrate you! That's how that story goes.

When we believe in possession we will misuse the energy of our consciousness in various ways. When we believe in possession we will desire. Desiring is imagining 'being in possession', then we create anxiety between here and there, as we worry if what we desire may not actually arrive in our life.

Once we do seemingly 'acquire' we learn to believe it is now mine. We will spend much of our time and energy thinking about how to ensure it or they 'stays with me'. Our consciousness will generate fear (insecurity) with increasing frequency as we believe some event or somebody may take away what we believe is 'mine'.

We will however just accept the fear as a natural feature of the package called life. But the big moment of unhappiness comes when inevitably what or who is with us has to leave. That's when we make our self sad. It's the 'habit of sadness' that, like all habits, eventually becomes a permanent feature within our consciousness.

It's the repeated creation of sadness that eventually becomes an almost permanent feeling of depression. It just means you have manufactured the emotion of sadness so frequently within your self that it just hangs there like a permanent cloud. Or it comes and goes with increasing frequency in what we call our 'moods'.

We know the cloud can be banished temporarily with some kind of stimulation or distraction. But it eventually returns, seemingly without invitation. What we don't notice is that you can only create a sense of loss and sadness if you are carrying the 'viral belief' that what you lost actually belonged to you, was possessed by you, in the first place.

Amazingly when 'it's time' for someone close to leave and we create sadness it means we had 'assumed possession' of that person. We didn't consciously think that. But we subconsciously believed that. In fact if someone had ever suggested that we tried to posses 'the other' we would probably reply, "Well of course I don't possess them." But deep in our consciousness we have been holding on to, attached to, dependent on, them. Probably for a long time. And that is as good as attempting to possess and believing 'they' are mine.

Then there are times when you won't need to believe that you personally have lost something or someone to feel sad. You can just watch others lose what they believe they have/possess and feel sad on their behalf. As we do! We watch the movie in which the characters are all sad because they believe they have lost something or someone, so what do we do? We sit and cry at the movie thereby strengthening our habit of creating and feeling ...sad!

With so many opportunities to be sad we learn to believe it's natural and healthy to feel this way sometimes. There seems to be no need to do anything about it. It's no wonder depression is so popular!

Where is all this 'possessing' and 'losing' happening in reality? Within our own consciousness. With the belief in possession there comes worry, which is fear, then sadness, which then turns into depression, or into anger at the world for taking away what is MINE!

It's no wonder we become so tired. It's no wonder stress levels are on the rise in almost every culture. It's no wonder we have a new set of diseases in many so called 'developed societies'.

There is only one way out of this emotional mess. And it is a mess, created entirely by our self, according to the beliefs we have inherited and given the status of truth in our own consciousness. And that is to 'see through' the illusion of possession. On the other side is the realization of the 'reality of the temporary'. The reality of non-possession.

We all seem to know deep down that nothing and no one stays forever. You do 'know' this don't you? The evidence, if you need it, is your own life and your relationships with everything and everyone. It's impossible to possess, hold on to, keep, make mine forever, anything or anyone. Obvious isn't it?

If you see the truth that nothing can be possessed it doesn't mean you just give up, give everything away and say well if I can't 'have' anything or anyone what's the point. Yes the belief in possession goes so deep into the consciousness of some they will 'think' this and start to believe life would be worthless and hopeless without 'ownership'.

But others have this penny drop very rapidly and they realize there is a tremendous freedom, a sense of liberation that comes with the acceptance of this reality.

Imagine you now know that you cannot ever own or possess anything or anyone. Yet people and objects, positions and possibilities, they still come to you. That is what life is always offering you. But now, instead of trying to hold on to everything and everyone, you let them come and stay in your life for as long as they want. And to go whenever they do. Without any attempt to keep.

You 'know' there is always a moment when every thing and everyone have to leave your life. But now you can't be forced to give anything up because you know it's not yours anyway. You 'know' this, so there is no fear of things going. No sadness when they do go. No anger. No tension in trying to protect and hold on. No more vicarious sadness as you watch the tears of others who still believe they have lost what they mistakenly believed they 'possessed'.

Can you imagine the peace that is restored to your life? Can you see how you are then free on the inside? Free of worry, free of frustration, free of sadness. All because you realize nothing, in reality, is ever yours.

Now you can see that every thing comes into your life for 'use'. Everyone appears in your life as an 'opportunity'. The opportunity to be creative. To create a relationship where every relationship is unique. Each has it's own colour, texture and perspective - metaphorically speaking.

"But how do I then define myself"? I hear you ask. You don't! You can't. Because you also know deep in your heart that you cannot define your self by what you don't have. And you don't HAVE anything.

So now you have to look a little more deeply and redefine your self as a free spirit, a peaceful person, a fearless individual, a compassionate soul, a source of love, pure awareness, helping others to free themselves from their illusion of possession. Free them from the sadnesses that you can now see they mistakenly create for themselves.

If you don't want to go down this road to restore this somewhat ancient but deep spiritual truth to your awareness, experiment with the following 'liberation philosophy' and see the difference it may make to your inner life. It goes very simply like this.

Every thing comes for use - now how best can I use this.

Everyone comes to give me the opportunity to be creative and to care - now what can I do, what actions can I create, to care for and about this person or these people.

Try this approach for a day while holding the insight that nothing is mine in the background of your consciousness.

Eventually you may, one day, fully realize the impossibility of loss.

Out there, beyond the beliefs in possession and loss, is the reality of your authentic happiness.

If you can see this and sense this you are on the road. But reading about it will make little difference. This is just a reminder. All of the content of this book is just a reminder of what you already know but have lost awareness of.

You won't really know it fully again until you do it, be it, live it - in the kitchen, in the office, in the car, everywhere. That may take a few days longer than it didn't take to build Rome!

Can you see it?

First the theory. Then the realization. Then the application.

What else is there to do? Everything else is delay!

LOVE

BEYOND BELIEF

If Hollywood had its way
You would have to search no more
It would be bottled every day
Available in every store

It's just become the fashion
To allude to love in a way
That it's something to do with passion
To be felt and indulged each day

If you don't there's something wrong
You're not part of the human race
There's a danger you'll never belong
So you better fix your face

Only then, you learn to believe
Your 'special one' will see
You are worthy of their attention
Saying 'You are the one for me'

And so you begin to imagine
The fulfillment of love will occur
Not realizing the myth of romance
Will turn your life to a blur

Love comes not from another
Wisdom humbly helps you to see
Yes of course you can receive it
But it's something you're meant to be

So waste no more time in your search
Or in waiting for 'them' to show
Just give of your self today
And true love you will start to know

Its beauty explodes from your heart
It never makes any demands
It radiates from your being
When you know it is what 'I am'

You have been brilliantly programmed to believe that love has to be acquired from another.

Have YOU bought into the myth of romantic love?

It's not easy to break out of this myth. Hollywood have done a brilliant job injecting into our consciousness the belief that love is only found when you find your perfect 'other', your soul mate, the one that's been waiting just for you. Apparently.

While we wish there to be such a 'special relationship', it seems many know, deep down, it is a myth. We know there can be magical feelings when we do connect with one other. We know there can be a kind of electricity, a chemical reaction, with another soul. That's when being together seems the most natural thing in the whole world. Even when 'they' are not present, perhaps hundreds of miles away, it still feels like they are sitting right next to us.

Sleeping, eating and meeting others in a focused state become ...challenging! Thinking about other important things ...difficult!

But when we do start to spend 24/7 with our special one it soon becomes apparent that there is a price to pay for what we call 'falling' in love. When the honeymoon period fades and the grind of daily life takes over with work and family and bills and washing and agreeing and disagreeing, then the scales tend to fall fast from dewy eyes.

That's often when we start to realize there is a deeper kind of love. A truer kind of love. One that doesn't see the faults and foibles of the other. One that instantly forgets any arguments. One that always maintains a benevolent vision and attitude towards the other. One that never seeks to try to possess or control the other and yet still supports the other. A love that endures is a love that has fewer and fewer expectations of the other, until there are no expectations at all. No dependency upon the other, yet always present when the other needs. Always appreciative no matter how small the others gestures.

The greatest love in any relationship arises when there is the realization that love isn't sourced from another but resourced from within oneself. Love is only known when it is brought forth from inside out in any one of hundreds of ways. Then the other is perceived not as a 'love interest' but a love opportunity. Not in an 'opportunistic' take advantage, sense. But an opportunity to be within a relationship in which there is the chance to create, give and receive lovingly and, as a result, rediscover the real meaning of love.

What does love mean to you? What is your belief about love?

Can you define love? Do you need to be loved? Is it really impossible to 'fall' in love? If so, why so? If not, why not?

If you have any hesitation in response to any of these question take it as an invitation to research and explore. Sometimes it is described as the highest currency of exchange within any human relationship. But what is 'it', exactly? Money changes hands. Does love change hearts? Does there have to be an exchange?

Imagine you are a 'love consultant' and you have been asked to give a presentation to 100 people on The True Meaning of Love. What would you say? How would you present it?

Consult family and friends. Get the conversation going. In between, give your self the time and space to reflect and ponder. Write down your thoughts. Notice when you are writing memories of other peoples beliefs. Those beliefs about love that you have already assimilated. Stop it!

Will you live your entire life without knowing the truth about love? Or...

Part THREE

Myths and Realities
about your SELF

Are YOU
Self Aware, Self Accepting, Self Controlled,
Self Esteemed, Self Respected,
Self Loved, Self Motivated?

Of course NOT!

In reality they are all impossible

Nice ideas, but based on a set of beliefs
that are not at all true!

But it's tricky to see this clearly.
Contemplate with me!

Ah Yes, the SELF!

There is a set of beliefs around the self that are misleading. They have arisen in the past few decades within the context of the increasing interest in spirituality and the many forms, facets and faces of 'personal development'.

There is a separate self. There is an entity called soul or spirit or consciousness or self, that is not made of the same energy as that of the body, the form, the physical material costume.

But only you can prove this to your self.

You will not 'know' for sure until you stop just believing it and realize it for your self. The practices of meditation and contemplation are the primary ways in which you can make the shift from just believing there is a separate self to realizing your self, for your self.

As you do you will also start to realize the illusions that have arisen around self-awareness and self-acceptance and indeed self-love. And why each is impossible in the truest sense.

It does no harm to continue practising what you believe is self-love, self-acceptance, self-control etc. In the process you will gradually become more aware of why they are all impossible to achieve. As you start to see clearly what you are doing within your consciousness it will gradually become apparent you cannot do or give anything to your self.

To help you see and realize this I've tried to explain in words in the following pages how to approach each of these 'beliefs' in order to help you move beyond them and to start realizing and 'knowing' what is true for you.

As I mentioned, words are always inadequate and can only ever point. They may trigger glimpses of the truth, or realities beyond the unrealities of belief. But only trigger!

If we are to know for our self we each have to go there and see for our self.

So let's go!

SELF AWARENESS

BEYOND BELIEF

Is it not time to become aware
Of being just pure awareness
No longer many selves
Only awareness, pure awareness

But who's aware of what
Or is it what's aware of who
Are you there or are you here
Where is here and there for you

When you are aware of being here
You'll find there is no there
You will see there is no then
And you are now nowhere

Ah yes, now here I am
Not then, not when, not never
Just fully present as 'amness'
In the here and now forever

But who is here
I hear you ask
To see no one
Now that's a task

To realize
There's no one here
Is the only way
Beyond the fear

So sit and be and watch
Then ask that tricky question
Who exactly is the watcher
Why is their no reflection

Such secrets, ancient and benign
Are revealed by this curiosity
In the moment when you 'know'
Comes the death of all verbosity

You may be carrying the belief that self-awareness is possible and indeed necessary to your awakening.

But, in reality, you cannot be aware of your self.

Terms such as self-awareness, self-esteem and self-motivation are what you might call the 'buzz terms' of the modern spirituality/self development/personal growth movements. Dr Google can give you access to a million insights on a thousand sites almost instantly.

All the terms above, found in almost any so-called spiritual book/treatise/seminar/process, have one thing in common. They are impossible to achieve. To believe they can be achieved is to be deceived! Here is why!

"I am learning to be more self aware", is what we may say after the seminar or the book. Yes you can be more aware of your thoughts, but only after you have created them. Yes you can be aware of your perceptions, but only a microsecond later when you look back on your perception. You can be aware of your intentions, but only those of a moment ago. But you cannot be aware of your self. It's the self that is being aware.

It's like that old analogy, can the eye see the eye, can the finger touch itself? Obviously not. But there is a paradox at the heart of this understanding. The self cannot be aware of the self because it's the self that is being aware. In truth the self is awareness itself. Sometimes referred to as consciousness. Yet, if the self is consciousness and perceptions and thoughts originated in consciousness, then they also originate in the self.

So while thoughts, perceptions, memories and ideas all seem separate from our self, they occur within the self. This matters, as any and all our suffering/stress/sorrow begins when the self ceases to be aware that is not it's own creation. It's when we lose our self in what we create that the ego is born and emotional suffering starts.

But it seems we won't notice this until we're ready. Between now and being fully aware of this, many realizations are necessary. The primary realization is that you are not a physical form. You are not even your brain. You are the being of consciousness, the energy that animates brain and body. How do you 'know'? You don't until you notice that you are not confined to the material dimensions of time and space. You can transcend these dimensions at will if you learn how to meditate. But the body you occupy cannot. It must always be in time and space.

Paradoxically the beginning of any practice of meditation simply makes you more aware of why you are not able to meditate! Not able to go beyond the awareness of time and space. This is necessary in the process of refining your awareness and your ability to become aware of 'the subtle'.

If you only practise meditation in order to relax that's OK. But ultimately it won't work until YOU start noticing what is happening in your own consciousness. That means seeing what YOU are doing i.e. 'creating', in your consciousness, that is making you feel unrelaxed. In other words you can't 'learn' to relax unless you unlearn all the things you are doing within your self that is making you feel unrelaxed. Relaxation is your natural state.

Does that resonate with you?

So who is this YOU, this I that is becoming more aware. Not of your self, but of what is originating, occurring, being created within ...YOU? You are, well, YOU! Which is no one really.

Any word is insufficient. You can use the word soul, or spirit, or consciousness, or self. It doesn't really matter. What matters is that you notice that it is YOU that is noticing. When you do you will notice you are awareness itself.

But you won't be aware of that in that moment. If you think 'I am awareness itself', in that moment your not awareness itself. You are not being your self. The 'thought' you just created has your attention and has you wrapped around its little finger... so to speak. Being lost 'in' thought is our most frequent habit. It also distracts, narrows and confines our awareness.

So unless you can be aware that you are awareness itself you cannot be aware of your self. And if you can, and many will say this is the purpose of meditation, you won't be thinking "Aha! Now I am aware of my self".

So, lets proceed with the other self-this and self-that, and see why they are also impossible and ultimately red herrings in what is sometimes called the process of awakening.

That said, for most of us the 'attempts' to be more self-aware, self-controlled etc. seem to be necessary stages we have to go through in order to 'wake up' fully to reality. In other words the effort of trying to become more self-aware, self-controlled, self-accepting, self-esteemed etc. seems to be necessary until you see for your self that they are impossible.

With the realization of impossibility comes a clearer and deeper awareness.

Clear? I thought not! Hang in there and stay interested if you can.

Clarity follows... eventually!

SELF ACCEPTANCE

BEYOND BELIEF

It appears to be recommended
All self judgment be suspended
That when you no longer consider
Your self to be a sinner
All guilt and shame is ended

From the wise there is an insistence
To terminate all resistance
If you go with the flow
Embracing all then you'll grow
And flower into full existence

They say you don't have to agree
Or condone all that you see
But if you can accept
With genuine respect
You will know the meaning of 'free'

But it's always good to be clear
Not believing all that you hear
There is only one aspect
You never need to accept
And yes that's your self, my dear

For you are the one that's accepting
Even when everyone else is rejecting
There is wisdom in this
You will find nothing amiss
You just have to be free of expecting

So try many times today
To embrace everyone in this way
Then you will discover
Why you need not recover
From whatever they do, it's OK

You may have been taught to believe that if you can just accept your self as you are, you will nullify all your guilt, shame and self-criticism.

But it doesn't work like that.

There is no need to accept your self. You can't anyway. Although, when you 'believe' you are self-accepting, it does seem to help! For a while at least!

"That's unacceptable", is often heard from the lips of the outraged or offended. They have yet to realize they have no choice but to accept whatever they condemn. What they are calling unacceptable has already happened and cannot be changed. So they have to accept it eventually. It's just a question of how long it will take to relinquish the rage and move out of resistance to the memory of what has already happened.

Acceptance of others actions does not mean you agree. It does not mean you condone. It just means you have realized that people will do what they will do. You have no choice but to accept it is done. And if you try to 'unacceptably anticipate' all that they are possibly about to do you are wasting your time and energy, which means wasting your life. Agree? Can you see it?

But what we are really interested in here is acceptance of your self. When you believe you accept your self what are you accepting exactly? That's a question that could keep most conversations going for a long time. Could the answer be no one?

Notice when you believe you are accepting your self you are just accepting what you have already thought, said or done. You are always accepting something in the past. They are memories. And 'you' are not a memory. You are not what you thought, said or did. You are you. Right here, right now.

You are the one who is doing the accepting. So how can you accept the acceptor? There is no subject AND object. That's why it's impossible to accept your self. So you can give it up.

Yes we do 'seem' to be in resistance to our self. But again look closely at what you are resisting and you will notice it's the version of you that said this or did that. It's a memory. It's the past. And you are not the past. You are here and now. Always and forever, here and now.

So the task is to accept the past i.e. what you have just said or done. Ultimately you will notice you have no choice. If you don't accept then you are in resistance, which means you are trying to change it. And the one thing in life you can never change is what has already happened. That's why it's just a matter of time before you do accept and 'move on'. That usually means forget it.

Practise on the outer world first. Just accept everything and everyone as they are according to how you find them. Notice when you don't, you are just making your self discontented and then mistakenly projecting responsibility for your grumpiness onto someone or something.

Once you master the art of accepting everyone and everything you will naturally realize you cannot and need not accept your self. Then all thoughts of, "Oh dear I need to accept my self more", will naturally disappear. Try it. You'll see!

There is another apparent paradox in all this. When you accept others and events as they are you are really accepting your 'version' of others and events, which exist entirely in your mind, in you. To accept others is to accept your creation of others, which is as close as you will come to accepting your self ...in a 'roundabout' sort of way.

In fact if you can fully accept the other as they are, you will notice how you are creating others and connecting with others with greater compassion ...within you. It goes something like this. Lets say your partner becomes angry with you and they start to blame you for how they feel (they have not yet read this book!). In such moments most people would go into resistance and start becoming defensive against the emotional attack and the accusations of their partner.

Whenever you are in resistance to anyone it's as if there is a disconnection. Any rapport comes to an end. You are taking what they are saying and doing 'personally'. You are interpreting it as an attack on you.

Imagine, instead of resisting and moving into acceptance. Imagine you don't take it personally. You can see they are making themselves very unhappy, they are suffering. Then projecting that suffering on to you. So instead of defending your self and trying to keep them out, which is resistance, you respond with compassion, which is born out of acceptance, which is love in action. Is that not what we would do naturally, if we saw a stranger suffering.

The moment you are able to move from resistance to acceptance is when you start to 'create them' differently in your own mind, in you. You can see their suffering, understand they are making themselves suffer, accept they are in that state, and you are therefore able to be more compassionate towards them. This in itself will help calm them and, if you can listen with that compassionate intention, it will allow them to dissolve their own unhappiness.

The hard part here is not taking it personally. Practise in your mind first. Imagine what this would look like and feel like. Create a scenario in your mind. Use memories from the past of where you see yourself responding with acceptance followed by compassion.

As you do you will become acutely aware that your emotional suffering that follows your resistance is entirely self created and you will start to see exactly why you are creating it. When you do see this clearly you will then always have the option of creating a different response, the accepting response.

So why do you find your self 'believing' you are not accepting your self enough? It's simply because others appear to not accept you. Whenever they blame or complain at you or about you it seems you are being rejected. So you create the belief that 'I am a reject'. You then use this belief to construct your sense of identity based on 'I am a reject'. This belief and it's consequent thoughts then generate feelings of dissatisfaction, discontentment. Then, when you hear someone talk about the need for self-acceptance you naturally lock on to it with the thought, "Yes that's what I need to do". You are really saying to your self, "Well I need to be accepted and no one else is accepting me so I might as well accept myself".

The real solution is to end the belief that you are a reject. And you don't do that by self-acceptance. You do that by understanding that it's not you that others are apparently rejecting. It's their version of you that they are creating entirely in their consciousness. It's their problem not yours. Not easy to see but once you see it you'll wonder why you didn't see it sooner!

Can you see it? Yes it's subtle. Sometimes. Not so subtle at other times.

Take a moment. Dip in and out of the paragraphs of this chapter again. Note down what you see and realize for your self. Then, when you're ready, see if you can explain it to someone else.

As you do you will start to realize you know more than you thought you knew!

SELF CONTROL

BEYOND BELIEF

We are great at fixing others
In our thoughts and conversations
Filled with shoulds and musts and oughts
We avoid internal observation

If only they would do (we think)
What we want or expect
We would then want to restore
Full regard and great respect

But they're not doing what you want
So you become so snappy
Believing it's always 'them'
Making you so damned unhappy

But if you stop and look and see
It is from this your stress arises
When 'they' don't be or say or do
You create a mini mental crisis

So relax and be liberated
From controlling others lives
It's not your job you see
Put away your mental knives

There's only one script to be written
That's your life with great coherence
But you won't be that creative
Till you end your interference

Chill out and let 'them' be
Sit quietly with your choices
Allow your heart to show
What's next without those voices

You don't even have control
Of your purest intuitions
They just arise to let you know
There will be a natural fruition

Most parents teach their children one particularly fatal belief when they shout 'control your self'!

But can you?

"Control yourself", said many mothers to many unruly children. "You need to learn to control your self", said many managers to other managers after they lost the emotional plot in the meeting. "I must learn to control myself better", we have probably all thought to our self after overreacting to someone else's words.

But can you? Can you control your self? If you are controlling your self what exactly are you controlling?

What seems an uncontrolled reaction is really just words and emotions that come tumbling out, often like bullets targeted at the other person or the situation. Or just as an expression of confusion in an exchange that has 'pressed your button'.

So it's not the self that needs to be controlled. It's what the self is creating. Whenever we 'react' verbally or emotionally it's always our creation. And the self is the creator not the creation.

Self-control is therefore code for 'be more mindful' of what you are saying and feeling. Control your creation. Not your self. It's impossible to control your self. The self is the controller.

Now here's where it becomes deep and subtle. As long as you are being your self you will never need to even think of doing what you can never do anyway, which is control your self. Only when you are being your natural self will what arises from you, the self, in the form of intention, perception, thoughts and words emerge in a natural, non-emotional, totally appropriate to the situation, way.

The reason we lose control of our thoughts and create emotional reactions is simply because we are not 'being our self'. It's a sign that we have lost our sense of self 'in' what we are not. We have lost our self in a habit or in a belief, or in a mental image in our mind.

In other words if you lose your temper at your child when they keep speaking while eating at the dinner table, it means you have lost your self 'in' the idea/belief they should not speak when eating. Subtle, isn't it. So it's not a question of 'control your temper'. It's a question of becoming aware that, "It's me that is lost in an idea/belief, which is being contradicted by reality out there at the breakfast table". Over which you have no control. But you are taking it personally, hence the emotional reaction. Only when you stop losing your self in what you are not (an idea or belief) will what arises from your consciousness, i.e. from you, be free of emotion.

In other words any apparent need for more self control just means there needs to be a restoration of the awareness of who 'I really am'. It's time to stop trying to force your ideality onto reality. But that will not happen as long as you are not aware that you are using your mental ideality to define your self. You won't stop doing it until you stop losing your self in your own ideas. And that really is subtle.

Yes it's all about the ego. The ego is created the moment we build our sense of self out of what we are not. It's the ego that reacts emotionally. That's why living in this world is like living on an emotional rollercoaster. Everyone learns to lose their self in what they are not e.g. the idea/images of what they have, what they do, where they live, where they were born, what they want, what they believe etc. This is the root cause of all uncontrolled reactiveness.

Our challenge then is not to be more in control. It is to free our self from the habit of reacting in an emotional way, which means uncontrolled way. That does not require self control it needs only self-liberation i.e. stop identifying with what you are not. Only then can you be your self. And when you are being your self there is no reactiveness. Then it doesn't matter what others say or do, you are not affected in any way.

You engage, but the manner of your engagement is relaxed and creatively appropriate. You cannot be offended or insulted so you never become upset. Emotional suffering becomes a relic of the past! Yet you are loving and contented in your ways of expression. There's a quiet joy towards everyone you meet and you are able to maintain an internal equanimity in relation to whatever happens in the world around you. When you can do this it is a clear sign you are making what is often referred to as 'spiritual progress', which just means you are 'waking up'.

Careful you don't create an inaccurate impression of what I have just said. Being free of emotional reaction is not a kind of flat lining way of life that's boring and dull. Love and joy, authentic happiness and serenity, do not come under the heading 'emotional states'. This is just another set of beliefs that need to be 'seen though'. Being unemotional does not mean being unloving or unempathic or uncaring. Quite the opposite. You cannot be caring, empathic and accepting unless you free of emotion. But we'll come back to that later.

But remember. Don't believe me! Next time you react emotionally see if you can notice who or what you are trying to control. It's all happening in your mind. Another paradox, while you are not your mind, your mind is in you.

Write down all the things in life over which you have no control. Carry the list with you and look at it occasionally. When you do, ask your self which of those things have I tried to control in the past day/week/month ...in your mind. Just with your thinking i.e. they 'should', they 'must', they 'have' to!

This enhances your awareness.

If you are not aware of the mistakes you are making in your consciousness then you can't correct them.

SELF ESTEEM

BEYOND BELIEF

When I lose my estimation
Of my intrinsic worth and value
I look for affirmation
From him and her and you

When it's not forthcoming
Or when I disagree
I make myself feel awful
Asking, "What's happening to me"

I learn to make this one mistake
Of seeking validation
From people, positions and possessions
Thus creating life's complications

But learning to remember
How unique I always am
I start to see my inner beauty
And begin to think 'I can'

Self esteem means realizing your value
But not in monetary terms
It's a deep intuitive knowing
Not based on anything you learn

It's always there deep down
This sense of a beautiful you
But being aware and knowing it
Requires love and attention too

Take a moment to sit quietly
Cultivate your introspection
Remind your self you are unique
And you will feel a new affection

One day you'll know that at the core
You are pristine and perfect
But to get there you will need
To meditate and reflect

Somewhere along the line of your life you have assimilated and created your version of the belief that you need high self esteem to live a happy and fulfilling life.

But's it's old non-sense!

The term 'self-esteem' was seldom on the radar thirty years ago. And look at it now. Lording it on the front cover of hundreds of books. Commanding huge fees for thousands of seminars. And attracting the attention of mostly the female fraternity, as that 'missing something' that is the cause of all those 'poor me' moments. Not forgetting they tend to be more honest about such feelings than the male fraternity. But the boys are getting in on the act too!

Take a moment and say the following to your self. "I esteem my self". Can you sense how ridiculous that sounds. Or "I have high self esteem". Also a little daft. What's high and what's low? Do you know what you really mean by 'high self-esteem'? Are you perhaps mixing it with our old friend the ego?

Either way you are probably trying to turn esteem into a belief. Impossible. Won't work. Why? You cannot esteem your self.

Esteem is short for estimate. When combined with the idea of value you begin to get the meaning of esteem - an estimate of value. Try estimating your value by 'thinking' about it. Go on try it! You'll start laughing after a while. Then wonder why you believed it was ever possible in the first place.

'How do I build my self esteem' is a question asked by many. You don't, because you can't 'build' it. Your sense of 'value' and your inner beauty requires rediscovery, not construction. But when you do rediscover it the last thing you are thinking is. "AHA! now I have found my self-esteem".

So how do you rediscover and know your value? How do you restore your awareness of your inner beauty? This means how do you liberate your self from the illusions found in beliefs such as 'I am not good enough, I don't have enough confidence, my character is irredeemably flawed and I am just too afraid to assert my self'.

Rediscovering and being aware of your uniqueness, beauty and value requires you recognize and drop all these stories that you keep telling your self about your self. Stories that are filled with beliefs that are not true. It's necessary to stop building a sense of identity out of your beliefs about your self based on your past experiences. Including what others said about you, to you, along with any memories of your apparent failures.

So the remedy is simple, in theory, but requires vigilance in practice. All you have to do is recognize each time you start telling stories about your self and say to your self, "This is just a story and I am not a story".

You are the creator of all these stories. Yes you got some help from others interpretations and beliefs. You took their help by recreating your versions of their interpretations and beliefs.

You probably learned to compare your self with others from your earliest childhood days. You have allowed the media to tell you who you are and who you should aspire to be and what you need to do to get there and how you are always not quite there yet and therefore always lesser than the ideal ...phew! All fictional stories.

You are both the creator and sustainer of all the stories about you. The 'I'm not good enough' story, the 'poor me' story, the 'I am a reject' story the 'I'm not capable' story, the 'I'm not a nice person' story.

When you 'run' these stories it's like sitting in the movies and believing what you see on the screen is real life. But it's obviously not. It's an illusion. In fact it's an illusion of an illusion.

So what is the 'true story' about you, you may ask. The answer. No story. You are not a story. You are you. And when you are being just you that's when the feeling arises, the knowingness arises, from within you, that is telling you the truth about you. It is a knowingness that you are enough, you are beautiful, you are, well, everything that you are!

But you are not thinking that. You are not smugly sitting with the idea, "Aha now my self esteem is back". You just know. It's a humble knowing'. It's an unbreakable knowing. It's a solid and unshakable 'knowing'. But it's not a story. It's not just another set of beliefs or memories.

You don't need to believe anything because now you know.

It's a 'knowingness'.

Restoring your awareness of your real and true state of being, from which comes your sense of value and goodness, starts with intuitively realizing it's already there. Deeply buried under all the stories. It's a state of being that's prior to all your thoughts about everything.

Sometimes, in quiet moments, when we are fully relaxed we forget all our worries and anxieties, there is a break in the 'inner clouds of thoughts and memories' and we glimpse this state and 'insperience' the feelings that arise from it.

You feel fulfilled, you feel life is both profoundly wonderful and you feel great gratitude. You don't think it, you feel it. As soon as you 'think it' the feeling is gone.

But then, before we can live in this state your habitual thoughts and the stories kick in again. They bubble up from memory, burst into your mind, you believe them and get lost in them ...again.

This is where vigilance comes in. Keep reminding your self 'I am not this story, I am not this story, it's just a story and I am not a story'.

You can speed this process. In other words you will start to notice the 'thought stories' faster if you regularly take time out for some form of meditative practice. This is the practice of allowing your mind to become quiet and ultimately silent. Not by forcing it, or willing it, but by watching, just watching what is arising in the mind and practising the awareness that I am not what is appearing about me in my mind. Realizing it's just a story.

Slowly at first, but surely in the end, you will uncover and liberate your true sense of self, free of all stories. Free of all the beliefs you have been habitually creating and using to define your self.

Does that make sense?

If so then begin now.

If not send me an email.

But read it again first. What, for you, is not clear?

SELF LOVE

BEYOND BELIEF

Stand in front of the mirror
Say I love you again and again
That's the advice we are given
To be free of our aching hearts pain

We are told with all sincerity
That if we make loves biggest fall
Just be in love with our self
And more lovers will come to call

But how can you fall into your self
Can love be discovered this way
Deep in your heart you know
It's known only when given away

Give what you want
And you'll get what you give
And loves secret
Will be revealed

It sits in your heart
It is what you are
It's your gift to the world
It can never be far

This is the greatest riddle
That must be patiently solved
It's your glorious return to love
When all your illusions dissolve

Only then can you be what you are
A source of love for all
Available for everyone everywhere
Then you're always going to The Ball

'I have to learn to love my self' is a belief heard and absorbed and given the status of truth by many. So it's not easy to see why...

... it's just not possible.

"Perhaps I have to learn to love my self more," is a common thought, arising in those who feel unloved. "Perhaps there is a course or a book on how to love my self", as they go searching for the 'how to' manual.

But you can't. It's impossible. There are not two you's! There is not an 'I' and a separate 'self' that the 'I' can love. If you really 'believed' there was, you would likely be in a psychiatric ward.

Say it quietly to your mind, "I love my self". Then ask which one is me, is it the 'I' or is it the 'self'. Or is there a third, called 'me'? There are not two or three you's. Only one. When have you ever heard 'one does love one'?

When someone says I need to love myself they really mean 'I believe I need love' and no one is giving it to me so I might as well get some from my self. So it's just part of the same search for love. And that's the real problem. Love cannot be found. As soon as you start searching you are looking in the wrong direction. In fact love cannot be looked for.

Why? Because it is what you are. But only when your consciousness, that's you, is in your highest and purest state. A state where there is no longer any desire or neediness. A state that is free of all attachment and dependency. Not easy states to be in, in a world where love is equated with attachment and dependency. A world where we learn to believe and think, "I need to be loved".

But you don't. Not even as a child. The child needs to see how to 'be love', not be loved. They will be loved anyway if they are in the presence of a parent who is 'being love'. But few parents are. Their mindset is more like, "You need to be loved by me or I need to be the one who loves you most or children need to be loved the best by their parents". All these thoughts arise into a behavior in which the child learns to believe that love has to come from someone outside, usually an authority figure. And that just creates dependency and neediness, and perhaps a life long search for love when they leave their parents or their parents leave them.

It's simple really! You can only know love when you are being and doing love from inside out. But only when nothing is sought, expected or wanted of the other. That's why knowing love is not as easy as a trip to the grocery store.

Yes you can receive love from others in many ways. But the moment you 'believe' that it's necessary to acquire and receive love in order to be happy in your self is the moment you forget that 'it' is what you already are. It's also the moment you become dependent.

You can only know love in its truest form when your consciousness is in its highest vibration. Then that energy, that vibration, may come from you as care, as compassion, as virtuousness.

Virtue is love in action. It's you in your highest human consciousness. You're not thinking 'I am so virtuous' or 'AHA so this is love'! But you are perceived by others as loving, as a source of love, in that moment. But only when there is no clinginess! No subtle desire for recognition. No attachment. No neediness. All of that has been cleaned out of your consciousness.

When you express your self in virtuous ways you are the first to feel the love that you are in that moment, as it flows from you into the world. In that moment you know your self as love. Only then do all thoughts of seeking love or loving your self disappear.

Why would you believe and think you have to love your self when you are being it and, in being it, knowing it is what you are? All beliefs about love become irrelevant in that moment.

It's unfortunate that most of the habits that we all learn at this time, in this grasping world, are contrary to loves ways. Wanting, keeping, depending, needing, attaching, having, are the most popular habits that ensure love is blocked, distorted and polluted. But it's just the way things are. The way they have evolved to different degrees in different places. All we/you/I can do is notice this, understand this and free our self from this.

Love is a word that describes the consciousness of every human being when it is vibrating and radiating at its highest level. But to know this for ones self requires seeing and dropping everything that pulls our consciousness into a lower vibration.

Once again that requires the practice of 'noticing' when and how we do that to our self.

Why not take a few moments at the end of the day and ask your self what were my unloving behaviors, thoughts or intentions today. When you reflect and remember them don't dwell on them just notice them and then forget them. Eventually you will start to notice them not in reflection but in real time. That's when you will see and start to remove what you are using to distort your own energy, your own consciousness, your 'self'.

The paradox of love is when you are it you know it but you don't 'think' you are it.

If you did you would not be love. You would be the idea of love. Probably trying to be the ideal.

And love is not an ideal.

It can only ever be real.

SELF RESPECT

BEYOND BELIEF

For any rhyme or reason
You decide to be offended
You are blind to the reality
Your respect ability just ended

You see your self as victim
And your ego is exposed
As you indignantly declare
How much you are opposed

"It's them it's them
That makes me feel this way"
As you decide you will reject them
Forever, from this day

Then others are condemned
For what they say or do
You cannot see their value
You think they're not for you

But it only has one meaning
That you depend upon 'the other'
For their acceptance and approval
Perhaps a lesson from your mother

Until the day it dawns
And at last you realize
"It's me, not them, that makes me feel
You now see with your real eye!

That's the moment you return
To the driving seat of life
You become the master of your fate
No more struggle, no more strife

Everyone that you encounter
Receives your great respect
No mater what they say or do
It's OK, as you don't expect

You have frequently heard the term 'don't lose your self-respect' so you have learned to believe it's possible and necessary to maintain respect for your self.

But it isn't necessary and it's not possible.

To bow down to anyone; to want something from anyone; to be unable to speak assertively to anyone; are all signs there is a lack of self-respect. Apparently.

You need to build your self-respect. You've lost your self-respect. You need to recover your self-respect. Are all the things we say to someone who clearly is not respecting themselves. Apparently.

But it's impossible to respect your self for the same reasons that you cannot love your self. There is not a subject and object in the word or idea or reality of the 'self'.

When you think about someone you respect what does that really mean? Does it mean you fear them, as many of us tend to mistakenly believe? You don't respect the bully, you fear them. The bully may say, "Respect me or else", but they really mean, "Fear me!" Fearing is not respecting.

When you respect someone it means you affirm the value, the worthiness and the goodness in the other. It means that regardless of that person's history, their beliefs and opinions, you value them. You care about them. You see their worth even if they cannot see it themselves. You acknowledge their 'innate goodness' even when they may have done or are doing something not so good in society's eyes.

What makes this really hard is 'judgment'. We learn to believe that others should act and interact to certain standards. We expect others to live up to those standards. And when they don't we judge them. We withdraw our recognition of their worth, their goodness. We may even say, "I don't respect them anymore".

Occasionally you meet someone who respects everyone equally, regardless of standards and expectations. We mostly find this disturbing to watch as we ourselves judge and think, "Can't they see how horrible and nasty that person is. They must be blind, etc.". We then judge the non-judger!

But it's as if this 'non-judger' has a vision of the other that allows them to know and interact with the other as if they are a source of goodness and value. It's as if they see their worthiness, regardless of what that other person thinks of themselves. Regardless of what the other person has done in their life.

If you can translate that back to your self and you will start to see the real meaning of self-respect. Do you know your own value? Do you know your own worthiness? Do you know your own goodness? If you do, and you don't forget it, then what you call your self-respect will stay intact and stable in all your relationships. No matter who is in front of you, you will not feel lesser or inferior, nor superior, in any way. You will never create thoughts about your self that would diminish your self.

We respect the rules of an organization because we know their value in sustaining the harmony within an organization. We respect the laws of the country because they help maintain balance and harmony in society. We respect the qualifications of a person because we know they have given their time and energy to gain training and knowledge that helps other people.

But in each instance we are the one who is 'doing' the respecting. There is a 'me', the respecter, and there is 'them', the respected. However you cannot do the same with your self. You can only know your own worthiness, know your value, know your goodness. If you don't have this 'knowingness' then it could be called a form of ignorance.

It's a knowingness that cannot be taught. One of the only ways to help someone cultivate it is to have them be in the 'presence' of someone who already has this knowingness within themselves. Then the one who is ignorant of their own worthiness, value and goodness starts to see it in themselves through the vision and attitude of the other.

But even that is just first base. If we are to know our own goodness, or own value, it is necessary to give of ones self. Only in the giving is the knowing cultivated. When you know your worth, your value, your innate goodness, then there is no need for the belief that I need to find, build, rediscover my self-respect.

Similar to self-esteem, when you know, all such beliefs about self-respect dissolve. You realize that any time I withdraw my respect from another is the moment I am saying to myself I cannot see their worth, their goodness, their value. But why are you creating them as worthless, as badness and valueless in your own consciousness? It's normally because you have lost that knowingness of your self, of your own value, within your self.

Notice when you feel good within your self you are more able to see the goodness of others. Now take that to the highest degree. Only when you reside in the awareness of your own worth, value and goodness, are you 'able' to create and hold others in the same way within your consciousness. Otherwise you will see them as unworthy and without value. If so it means you have withdrawn your respect for them.

Can you see it? Do you get it? It's deep. It's subtle. It appears to be an elusive knowingness until you stop and allow your self to be aware of what you are putting in the way.

Yes it's those pesky beliefs again!

Stop. Reflect. Notice. Realize.

SELF MOTIVATED

BEYOND BELIEF

What moves you
Out of bed each day
Is it just the money
Is there another way

To make things happen
To get up and go
To leave your mark
To create your flow

Is it from the outside in
That you are energized
Or from inside out
That your inspirations arise

Likely is the moment
Of your self you will ask
What's the point of it all?
What is the real task?

Why am I here? What am I to do?
With this gift called life
How can I get through
Without the struggle or the strife

Then one day it dawns
It's not just about 'me'
Around me there are others
Aha! Now I see

I see us all together
As we co-create
This life, this epic journey
A collective co-created fate

When you bring your best
To all your interactions
From your heart arises
Life's real satisfactions

Are YOU self-motivated?

Many believe they are but have not yet realized they're not really!

When we watch someone being consistent, getting things done without the need for cajoling or checking we usually say, "Well they're just so self motivated". But are they?

It's an age-old argument. Are you motivated from outside in or from inside out. Is human motivation extrinsic or intrinsic? Even when we think it's intrinsic it's usually not. Here is why?

When you find you are self-motivated to do anything, look closely within and you will likely notice your old friend 'desire'. The reason you do almost everything is out of personal desire. You get the job done, you go to the movies, you plan the project, you help others, you work hard to make money, you spend hours in your garden shed potting plants. (perhaps!) They could all look as if they are driven by a natural enthusiasm but are they not just actions driven by desire?

It's not right or wrong, good or bad. It's just interesting to ask that question in our enquiry into motivation. What about you?

The root meaning of the word motivation is 'move'. What moves you? What gets you out of bed and out of the house in the morning? Is it just the money? Is it for some deeper purpose? Is it because you care about someone or some thing? Look closely and you will likely discover that you are motivated by something you want. Whatever it is, it means you are desire motivated. Especially if it's the desire to avoid something, like poverty, or someone, like your family!

That's also not right or wrong in any way. It's how the vast majority of us will live our entire life. Moved by desires, large and small. But there is a deeper source of motivation. It's called 'creativity'. Being creative is the ultimate purpose of human consciousness. Two reasons. Notice what you are doing all the time. You are thinking. To think is to create. Everything begins with the creation of thought. Your entire life will unfold according to your own thinking.

Now, can you get a measure of your sense of fulfillment and satisfaction in the process of being creative compared with fulfilling a personal desire. Is there a greater feeling of satisfaction/fulfillment when you are creative or when you acquire a long awaited object you have always wanted. Which one is deeper? Which one lasts longer?

You will find the 'creative process' wins hands down. But there is another dimension called context. It matters in what context in which you are a creative being ...being creative. Creativity in this sense is not about painting, or writing, or poetry etc. Although they obviously bring their own kind of fulfillment and satisfaction.

It's in the context of our relationships that we find our way back to the deepest creative impulse. Relationship is both the context and the continuous opportunity to be creative. When you are creative in that context it brings about the deepest feelings of satisfaction and fulfillment. But as soon as you bring a personal desire into the process it dilutes those feelings and dissatisfaction will inevitably arise. Is that true for you?

When you are motivated from 'inside out' that's when the energy of you is moving naturally without personal desire. It's when you give the gift of your self to something, perhaps the development of a task or a relationship, as opposed to wanting and receiving a gift from someone else.

When you are moved only by personal desire your inner world tends to shrink and be defined by the object of your desire. You are vulnerable to disappointment. Whereas when you are moved by your own creativity you tend to stay open, expansive and flexible, ready to try new things, receive input around how to improve your creative process. There will be no disappointment. Only an interest in how to do it or be it or give it better.

Once again being driven by personal desire is not wrong. As the energy of you moves from inside you and out into your endeavors it's just that 'desire energy' is not arising from the deepest level of you. Can you see it?

When you are motivated by personal desire you will inevitably find your self feeling unfulfilled and dissatisfied eventually. In fact it's desire that gets 'in the way' of your deepest intrinsic motivation. When you are moved by your own creativity, from inside out, it's the most natural thing in the world. When you no longer want any particular thing for your self, that's when your creativity is consistently available to every one. Sometimes it's called love. But not Hollywood love and not procreativity!

The more you exercise your creativity the greater your own sense of satisfaction and the more you sense others valuing both your creativity and you. Not that you need it. You don't when you know your own creative capacity. But it still 'arrives'. Does that concur within your insperience?

When you consciously make your self available you will start receiving invitations from unexpected sources. And when you respond creatively to each you will notice a feeling of fulfillment and satisfaction that surpasses all other feelings. It's not a high that leads to a low. It's not an upper that results in a downer. It's a deeper feeling that sustains itself.

It's those moments when you meet and respond to life as it arrives in front of you. A friend comes to you in a state of severe emotional suffering. You are able to create your self as a patient listener with an empathic attitude that allows them to clarify their own story and, as a result, it lessens their emotional suffering. You are creating the response that is needed in that moment.

You want nothing for your self. The result is a feeling of equanimity, a quiet peace. There's a subtle joy in your heart that arises as a result of you creating the capacity to give of your self in that way. In a way that helps your friend recover.

Even top sports people while being in a competitive environment will know this feeling. Yes they 'want to win'. And yes that brings one kind of satisfaction when that desire is fulfilled. But the deeper feeling arises out of the process whereby they created the fitness and stamina of their body. They created and fine-tuned the skillfulness of their play.

They created their everyday relationships with coaches and colleagues. Winning is just the result of such constant, consistent, day-to-day creativity.

Unfortunately our formal educations tend not to recognize this spark that lives within every human heart. In fact those who do recognize and follow a path that might grow that spark into a fire tend to be seen as mavericks or rebels. They become estranged in a social context that tends to emphasize and direct us towards acquisitiveness rather than creativity.

How about you?

Have you ever felt and been moved by your own creative sparkiness? If not it awaits your rediscovery.

When will you give it full expression?

When will you allow it to bounce you out of bed in the morning?

Part FOUR

Being Beyond the most Popular Beliefs

By now you have probably surmised there are many more than 30 beliefs that you have assimilated and are using to sabotage, if not kill, your self.   If only there was enough space. But then the book would probably require it's own transport.

Here are 16 more that may encourage and feed your reflections, contemplations, ruminations and realizations. Those practices are, after all, essential if you are to become a being beyond belief!

POSITIVE THINKING

BEYOND BELIEF

Always look on the bright side
So those sunny thinkers say
Be positive and spread goodness
Each and every day

But misery is not negative
You may one day discover
It's just a temporary aberration
When you forget to be a lover

It's a mistake that happens inside
To your thoughts and to your feelings
Dark emotions are the sign
That it's time to do some healing

If you can sink back in
To the heart of your own being
That's where you'll find the key
To realign your thinking

Yes your thoughts arise off center
Because beliefs are never true
But if you can just be super quiet
Thoughts and feelings arise anew

That's when you rediscover
The true nature of your being
And if you go right to the core
There's a secret that's worth seeing

There's neither positive nor negative
Within your consciousness
But we believe in this polarity
That's why we're in a mess

Within your being forever
No duality is found
Just an infinity of vibrations
That makes your world go round

So you believe it's good to be positive, you believe you are or would like to be a 'positive thinker'.

But it's just never going to happen. It can't!

There is no such thing as 'positive' thinking? Thoughts are created in consciousness and in consciousness there is no duality. There is no positive or negative. So what does positive thinking really mean?

There is duality all around you in the material world 'out there'. Up and down, left and right, hot and cold, here and there. There is a positive pole and a negative pole in the material universe. But duality disappears where thoughts originate - in consciousness.

Thoughts arise in the mind and the mind is a faculty of your consciousness, which is you. They arise from inside out, mostly shaped by memory. They only 'seem' to sometimes come from outside in. When you listen to and consume the thoughts of others you are creating your own 'thought versions' from the words that re-present their thoughts/ideas etc. What appears to be 'outside in' is still 'inside out'. You are still the creator.

Why is a positive thought to one person a negative thought to another? 'The currency is going to lose its value' is a positive thought to foreign exchange dealer but a negative thought to a stockbroker. Or perhaps vice versa.

'I am a great dictator' is a positive thought to the dictator but a negative idea to those being dictated to. 'All criminals should be punished' is probably a positive thought to most of the public but a negative thought to the criminal.

You could smile and laugh as you think and say, "I hate you", or you could frown and growl as you think and say, "I love you". You are feeling and sending a lower vibration of energy while thinking and saying something apparently positive. And vice versa. Now what's positive and what's negative? Neither is either! They are just thoughts and feelings.

"I am positive I cannot do that" - positive or negative? Neither!

Life in Black and White

But it's hard to escape this dualistic trap. The world 'out there' is dualistic by nature. We see and describe the world around us in terms of opposites. Our language then becomes polarizing as we couch everything and almost everyone in oppositional descriptions. That then becomes a habit that we transfer into our descriptions of events within our consciousness. Our own thoughts 'seem' to become dualistic. Our conversations become black and white, 'either or' in their structure. Freedom from this habit begins only when we start to consider the 'quality' of our thoughts as opposed to the polarity of our thinking. This takes us into slightly deeper territory.

Prior to your thinking is your state of being. Your thoughts are shaped and arise according to your state of being. There is a generally recognized true and natural state of being within us all. Usually described by words like 'peaceful, loving and joyful'.

But just 'believing' this doesn't make it so. We each need to see, feel and know this for our self. You can only do that when you cultivate a deeper awareness of the inner world of your consciousness through the practice of some kind of meditation and/or contemplation. But lets assume you have done that and you have realized the true underlying nature of consciousness, of you, is peaceful, loving and joyful.

These are not positive aspects of your nature. They 'are' your nature. Within the reality of your consciousness they have no opposites. Only varying degrees of quality. These words (peaceful, loving and joyful) are words that describe the vibration of your consciousness AND what you will feel when you are in those states of being. They 'describe' the underlying and ever present nature of the self! We simply lose our awareness of them i.e. our capacity to be in those states.

But remember, as soon as you think either 'I believe that' or 'I don't believe that' you are back in the 'dualistic trap'. When you decide to neither believe or not believe, you are then 'open' and able to see for your self, know for yourself, if this is 'true' for me or not. That is, if you're interested.

Aligned Thinking

When you're thinking arises from, and is shaped by, these states of being you could say your thoughts are true, they are accurate. They are 'aligned' to the core of you. When you are 'in' your true state of being you will notice that your thoughts follow your feelings. They are shaped by your feelings. They crystalize out of what you are feeling. Albeit quite fast! In a peaceful state of being you feel calm and your thinking is then naturally peaceful and calm in its quality.

When you are in a loving state of being you will first 'feel' that lovefulness, which will shape your intention as you act. Your thoughts will be shaped by, and arise out of, that state.

The thoughts that arise will be 'accurately aligned' with your true nature i.e. the 'trueness' of you. Not positive or negative, just aligned i.e. shaped by your true, core state of being. But if you are not 'in' that core state your thinking will be 'misaligned', not the opposite, but 'misaligned', to some 'degree' or other.

Misaligned Thinking

When your state of being is distorted then the thoughts that arise are misaligned, they are not as accurate. What distorts your state of being? Any form of attachment or dependency. Attachment takes place within consciousness. It can be attachment to things, in which case it's your idea/image of the object to which you are attached. Or it could be to people, in which case it's the idea/image of a person. Or it could be you are attached to your beliefs. The main sign that this is happening is you will think first and then feel. What you will feel is 'emotional' disturbance. You will feel emotional as a result of your thinking.

It happens fast. When someone says something you don't agree with you immediately think either 'that's not right' or 'I disagree'. That's because you are attached to your belief. Then follows the emotion such as irritation or anxiety. This is not negative. It just means your thoughts are no longer aligned with your true nature, your trueness, and the price you pay is an emotional disturbance of some kind.

This is all quite subtle and our emotional reaction seems so instant and overpowering that it's hard to see it is triggered by our own thought. It won't bother you for most of your life until the emotion becomes just too frequent, too intense or it leads to some kind of violent action. That's because all emotion is a form of suffering. Love and joy are not emotions. Again that is not easy to see after a lifetime of being taught to 'believe' they are.

Emotional Price

Here is a simple example. Imagine you meet someone for the first time who is struggling with a problem with which you have some experience. You have no preconceived belief about that person. So you feel quite open and warm towards them, which is coming from your true loving nature. From that 'feeling' comes the 'thought' that you would like to offer them help. So you say, "How can I help you". You went from state to feeling to thought to words to action.

Now let's say you are still carrying, within your consciousness, two of the most commonly held beliefs that a) other people are responsible for your happiness and b) it's good manners to say thank you. But they don't say thank you after you help. They mumble something, look away and then walk away.

In a millisecond those beliefs kick into your consciousness and you generate the thought (judgment), "How dare they almost ignore me and not appreciate my gesture". This is followed fast by the emotion of anger in the form of upsetness. You are emotionally upset. That was not a negative thought just an 'inaccurate' thought as it is not arising from your true peaceful and loving nature. You lost the plot because you were attached to those two beliefs. You went from state to belief (attachment) to thought to emotion.

The signal of this inaccurate and unaligned thinking is the emotional state that follows.

But it happens so quickly. You have lost awareness of the truth, that no one is responsible for your feelings (including the emotions that you create and feel) and that manners are just 'personal' standards to which we each become attached, or not as the case may be. Everyone has different standards/manners. In some cultures they never say thank you for anything but no one is ever offended.

Now, if those beliefs (around responsibility and manners) had not kicked in you would still be in your true peaceful and loving nature. You would still be 'feeling' warmth and acceptance towards the other. Your thoughts would probably sound something like, "Oops, I didn't quite understand what they just said". And you probably would have said something like, "Sorry I didn't quite catch that, could you say that again, thanks". In other words you would be 'feeling' acceptance first then the 'thought' to seek understanding follows.

You can test this everyday if you take a few moments to reflect after any encounter with another person. You will see it's not a question of positive or negative thinking. It's a question of did you remain within your true nature or did an old belief, habit, perception, kick in and knock you out of center, out of your natural state. And, as a consequence, you made your self suffer emotionally.

Are You Forcing it!

We have all heard, perhaps a thousand times, that most popular cliché, "But you have to be positive". So it becomes a belief that it's not only possible, it's necessary. But here's another simpler reason to get out of the habit of believing this belief. See if this is true for you.

Do you ever feel as if you are stuck in the tension of opposites? It's when you believe you are thinking something negative 'like this', and you believe you 'should be' thinking something more positive 'like that'. Simply because you have absorbed the belief that you SHOULD always 'be positive'. But you have probably decided that you have a habit of thinking 'I am always a bit negative'. Now you are caught in what is known the 'tension of opposites'. I'm here but I 'should' be there! I am being negative but I believe I should be more positive. But it's an illusion.

It's false because it's all happening in your consciousness where there is no positive or negative. In the meantime you beat your self up for having what you believe is a negative thought. If you have ever been on a positive thinking seminar you are probably now thinking (believing) that because you have just had a negative thought you are a failure, and you are going to attract some awful people, and something equally awful is going to happen to you as punishment for being so negative.

Phew!

All because you 'believe' it's possible to think negative and positive. This can then keep you stuck in a kind of 'continuous mental tension' of opposites almost your entire life. You will probably do far too much thinking. Including thinking about thinking!

You may even start to try to force your self to think positively, thereby resisting what you perceive as your negative thinking. Resistance and force then become internal habits within the energy of your consciousness. Suppression must follow, which also becomes a habit. So it's no wonder anxiety builds up inside. It's no wonder that 'resistance and force' start to emerge in words and behaviors within the context of your relationships. It's no wonder we then can't understand why some people just 'back off'. Crazy isn't it.

All the while there is a way out or, more accurately, a way back. And that's returning to the underlying core nature of your being. At the core you are pure peacefulness, pure lovefulness, pure joyfulness. But you've been sabotaging that with your beliefs and belief systems - the ones you have learned and the ones you have created. It doesn't matter what the beliefs are. Any and all beliefs will be a form of sabotage, pulling you out of your trueness.

When you are in your true and natural state of being you don't need to believe anything. On the way back to that state you may see for your self that there are no right or wrong beliefs! (duality again). It's the attachment to any belief that pulls you out of your true state of being. But that's another seminar.

From Theory to Reality

If you can see this in theory now, perhaps it's time to realize it in the reality of your own being. Perhaps it's time to allow your self to become fully aware of your true underlying nature. To invoke it. Be it. Experiment with it. Re-learn to trust it. Not just believe in it, but to 'know' it for your self.

Only then can you, will you, unlearn the beliefs that perhaps you are now starting to see are in the way of you being ...you! Some times this is called the spiritual journey. It's just that you don't go anywhere. Others call it awakening. It's just that you are not asleep, just unaware. Some call it self-transformation. It's not that you were not your self, it's just that you are in the habit of 'losing your self' in your beliefs, memories, images, ideas etc. but had no idea you were doing so.

All you need to do is notice that it's the 'belief' in positive and negative thinking that is at the root of so much of your thinking. Then challenge the belief with the question - is that true? When you realize it's not and when you realize you don't need that belief you will naturally let it go.

You will stop using the belief to support or define your self. You will step off the ledge of belief and find your self flying freely and joyously in the air of your own being.

Metaphorically speaking!

FREEDOM

BEYOND BELIEF

So you think you're free
To do just what you please
Roaming near and far
Blowing bubbles, kicking leaves

But behind this old illusion
That you're a liberated spirit
You are trapped in a story
And you'll likely have to kill it

It's a movie that you run
On the screen of your mind
Sometimes you're the star
That you're trying to find

But you are not a story
You're the creator, as you'll see
If you can realize this
Then you're almost free

Yes your life seems like a movie
With it's own conclusion
But you'll always continue
Beyond the last illusion

Step back from that screen
And you will likely find
The insight that you're not
What is on your busy mind

That's a kind if liberation
From a thousand little lies
Tasting this new freedom
A great relief you will sigh

It's only a free spirit
That knows just how to die
Only a being beyond all beliefs
That 'knows' how to fly

We learn to believe that we live in a free world, a free society. So we believe this is enough to believe we are free.

But it's not ...enough!

You can never be or feel truly free when you are trapped. But no one is ever trapped by anyone else. Your government cannot trap you. Your parents cannot trap you. Your boss or colleagues cannot trap you. Your job cannot trap you.

But you can use all of the above to trap your self. You only ever trap your self. You only ever relinquish your own freedom.

Freedom is not a state dependent on culture or law, on your ability to buy, fly, do or say anything. Freedom is a state of being that enhances the wisdom of your intellect and never agitates your mind.

Are you trapped in what you do? Many are because they believe they are what they do. Are you trapped in another person? Many are because they believe they cannot live happily without that person. Are you trapped in what you have? Most people are, as they believe they cannot survive and thrive without their possessions. Are you trapped in your beliefs? Almost everyone is, as they cannot imagine life without their beliefs. Some are so trapped they may simply kill others with differing beliefs because they believe that is the right thing to do.

If you are trapped you are lying to your self. Or more accurately, you are creating lies and then believing them!

Each of the above traps is not laid for us. We create and enter them our self. Seldom noticing that we do so. Even those who believe they are freedom fighters are trapped in the belief that they are not free. They have yet to realize that while it's possible to trap someone's body in a room it is impossible to trap their mind, their spirit, their 'self'. They do that, we all do that, all by our self!

That's why real freedom is so close and yet so far. We will spend our life trapping our self, sacrificing our freedom, without realizing it. We won't notice the connection between being trapped by our self and all our moments of all unhappiness, stress, sorrow etc.

Every morning, when we wake up we rebuild our own prison. Using our beliefs about people, possessions, pay, privileges, prestige and our position as 'bars'. We construct our prison cell. We sentence our self to life imprisonment. Then we spend most of our time and money either complaining how trapped we feel or on trying to find ways to escape. But we don't really escape; simply relieve the feeling for a while.

Freedom only really occurs when you decide not to lock your self up. Strangely people become comfortable in their cell. Unhappy, but weirdly comfortable, in their unhappiness. Breaking out and being truly a free being is frightening for most.

To do so they may have to accept full and absolute responsibility for their life. They may have to break a few dependencies. They may have to see themselves and others differently. They may have to change what they do for a material living. They may have to downsize their life. Have you ever done any of that?

Fear is always the sign of those who have made themselves unfree.

Evidence of the Unfree

The so-called terrorist is just a very frightened being who is trapped in the belief that other people and the world have made their feelings of fear and anger. They suffer and attribute their suffering to others. They believe vengeance is necessary to make others feel the same. They get to practice on a few video games and then some will step out into the reality of public life, vent their anger, and enact what they believe is their revenge.

They have not yet realized they are trapped in a story for which they are responsible in their own minds. They have not yet realized they make themselves suffer. They cannot yet see they have made themselves a slave to the object of their hate.

That's what hate does. You trap your self in the object of your hate in your own mind and turn your self into a slave. Who has ever been happy being a slave?

The freedom fighter is trapped in a mental story filled with beliefs that they are not free and someone else is responsible. Little do they realize and understand real freedom is only restored when they stop running their mental movie called Fighting My Way to Freedom!

The businessperson is trapped in their cell known as 'my business'. Frightened that their competitor will get to the marketplace first and be more successful. They create a story in their mind of likely failure. They lose themselves in that story. They lose their freedom of spirit. They make themselves suffer with feelings of stress and pressure. They may even begin to employ questionable business practices in order to avoid the 'imagined' outcome of their own fictional story of possible failure, loss and poverty.

Most parents are not free. They are trapped in the story they create about their relationship with their children. They worry. They 'imagine' what might happen. They create a mental movie with their imagination. Then run the movie in their minds, trap themselves in the movie, and make themselves suffer.

Trapped in such stories they are not free spirits. Their children then learn to do the same. By doing so they even believe that by creating 'worry stories' they are being caring. It's a powerful and captivating delusion.

The Freedom Secret

The most accurate word for all this, the most common mistake we all learn to make within our consciousness, is 'attachment'. When we lose our self 'in' what we create in our own mind, that's attachment. Then, when something happens to what we are attached to, it 'feels' like it's happening to 'me'. It's obviously not. But we will imagine it so well it will feel real anyway!

This is why there is no solution! There is no method or technique to become truly free. There is no formula. No quick fix.

The only way back to being a free spirit is to notice how and when you are making your self unfree. Noticing all the traps you lay for your self and unwittingly enter every day. Only curiosity and sustained interest can help. It's a process. It takes time. It's progressive. It's messy.

That said, it seems more and more people are beginning to make the connection between a messy world 'out there' and the habit of believing 'I am trapped'.

It's beyond politics and democracy, beyond culture or the way a society operates. It's beyond any of the ...'isms'. They can never be freeing for the human spirit. All they generally offer is another set of beliefs that you can use to build another cell.

What do you think, see or feel? What are 'the cells' you like to inhabit on a daily basis?

What would your life look like if you were truly free? Take your time with that one. It's a BIG question probably requiring much contemplation.

Let's meet in the shade of that big tree, on the hill, by the lake, on a nice warm summers evening, and discuss it!

TIME

BEYOND BELIEF

Glancing back
And looking ahead
Our favorite pastimes
Even in bed

Lost in worry
We like to fret
Then filling our mind
With cherished regrets

There'll be more time tomorrow
Is a comforting thought
Until we arrive there
And notice that there's not!

Then we learn to believe
If we accelerate our rush
We'll save time for later
The other side of the crush

Yet there's no such thing
As time they say
Just clocks and watches
Ticking all day

When 'this moment' is known
Time disappears
Then being fully present
Is the end of all fears

That's when you know
No 'things' trapped in time
Can remain the same
And they're never mine

If the truth could be told
There is only now
Some say this is Zen
Others call it the Tao!

You probably believe that time is a commodity, a resource, that can be managed and used in a controlled way.

IT isn't and you can't!

You can't capture it, stop it, save it or lose it. Time is not a thing, it's not an 'it'! Yet we think, speak and act as if it's a commodity, a resource, a 'something' that can be accumulated, saved and spent. Three illusions (beliefs) about time virtually run our personal worlds - time will 'run out'; we can 'save' time if we hurry; and if we wait there will be 'more' time later!

We will talk of being 'pushed for time' then, a few breathless moments later, we are rushing to 'meet a deadline' while confessing that we don't know where we will 'find the time'. But time is not found. It is created.

Time is a perception. More precisely, **time is your 'perception' of the space between events or the space in which an event begins and ends.** We are the creators of our perceptions so we are the creators of our time. The awareness of the passing of time is a natural, personal 'insperience'. Just as a canvas holds a painting so time is the canvas upon which we will paint the journey of our life.

So why do so many of us create a frantic time driven lifestyle? How do some of us (you know who you are!) seem to become slaves to time? Why did we start to mistakenly believe time runs out, time can be saved and there will be more time tomorrow? It all started way back when!

Once upon a time, long long ago, there was a young and brilliant carpenter. One day he built the most exquisite box. On the box he painted the most beautiful face and two perfect hands. That night, at around midnight, he went up into the forest, high in the mountains.

There, he whispered to TIME saying, "If you enter this box I can promise that you will control almost every human being on this earth". After a moments hesitation TIME replied, "Are you sure?" To which the carpenter replied, "Absolutely certain. They will think they are controlling you, but it will be you that controls them. I guarantee it". And so TIME accepted his offer and entered the box. The young carpenter returned down the mountain to his home and placed the box in the middle of high shelf so that all could see its face. And he called that box a clock!. It would not be long before the clock was mistaken for TIME itself and everyone would look to the face of a clock to guide their life.

Every time we think about time we tend to look at some form of clock somewhere. We organize our life around periods of 'clock time' and synchronize our movements according to the positions of the little hand and the big hand! We don't realize we look and refer only to a machine. We are unaware we are creating a false concept of time.

Clock time is not real time. In order to **quantitatively 'measure' our perception of the space between events or the space in which an event happens,** we invent seconds, minutes and hours as our units of measure. Being 'time conscious' is, for most of us, being 'clock conscious'. But it's a mistake. We invented and created the clock as one of our first machines. Today, many of us are slaves to our own creation.

So what is 'Real Time'?

Events in the world 'out there' are stimulations that register in the world 'in here' i.e. within your consciousness. Any stimulation, if repeated for pleasure, will eventually become addictive. As any drug addict will testify, more stimulation is gradually required to deliver the same effect.

The primary addiction almost all of us share is the stimulation of our consciousness 'in here' by events in the world 'out there'. Those events might include other people, movies, work achievements, family, the information and images delivered by our 'personal gizmos' and many other things! It's different for different people.

Gradually many, if not most of us, will try to 'up the dose' of event stimulation. Hence a growing desire for a 'faster' way of life and our collective preoccupation with speed. We become addicted to speediness, which is just an addiction to the stimulation of more and more events in a shorter space of time. Speeding up our life is essentially closing the space between events by consuming more 'event stimulations'.

Our relationship with technology is a classic example. When your computer 'hangs' notice what happens to your teeth as you grrrrr! for a few moments! You create the feeling of irritation or frustration, perhaps even anger, if it happens frequently. You are frustrated because you are not getting your fix of 'event stimulation' that you've come to expect and depend on from the machine through the screen. If the new model of phone or laptop is not quicker, slicker and able to supply you with more events, faster than its predecessor, it is deemed to be a backward step and not worth the money!

The Grammar of Life

Now this is where it gets 'interesting'. Just as punctuation marks are a natural characteristic of a good sentence, so too events themselves are like the punctuation marks in the long unending sentence that is your lifetime.

Punctuation in the right place within a written sentence allows the sentence to become meaningful. Using the sentence as a metaphor for our life it's in the space between the punctuation i.e. between life's events, that we 'ascribe/create' meaning. It's not the actual event that gives you the deepest meaning. It's in the space between the events in which you 'create the time' to 'ascribe' meaningfulness.

It's in that space/time that we consider, explore, understand, savior and thereby create our own 'personal meaningfulness'. This happens through a process of reflection and contemplation. The created meaningfulness that arises, which includes many subtle feelings, then informs our decision-making processes as to how and where we will use our attention and energy in what we call the future.

But, and here is the big but, if we are addicted to the stimulation of events themselves and we are always looking to increase the speed and frequency of events (i.e. trying to cram more events into our consciousness) then we are reducing the space between events where we do our meaning creation. The outcome? An increasing sense our life is becoming less meaningful.

We also reduce our capacity to 'see significance' during the events themselves. We are just busy with the thrill of the event itself. It all results in the tendency to race across the surfaces of life, find less and less depth and meaning to our life, which then diminishes our sense of satisfaction and fulfillment in life.

It's as if we need to create 'the time', which in consciousness is the same as 'the inner space', to consider, reflect and contemplate, in order to create meaning and therefore a meaningful life. That's why the exact meaning that you create of any event will always be unique to you. Otherwise we would all be clones.

In essence, it's not life's events that give you meaning it's what you do with those events within your consciousness, during and between the events themselves, that generates meaningfulness. The more addicted to the stimulation of events you become the less 'inner space' you have to 'make meaning' in your life. It's as if you are trying to make your written sentences out of just the punctuation marks, which would of course make a sentence meaningless!

This is reflected in the collective superficialization and loss of depth in so many areas of life that we see today. Hence the absence of meaningfulness in many peoples lives, perhaps most especially, the young! They have arrived and grow up in an already 'event accelerated' world. Hence the explosion in the number of people with some degree of 'attention deficit disorder'. This shows up as an inability to sit quietly, reflect, contemplate, create and extract the 'juice of meaningfulness' from what has happened and is happening. That's the 'juice' we all need to make future decisions about how we will create and live our life.

Consciousness, time and meaningfulness are all inextricably linked.

Types of Time

There are four kinds of time. Nature's time, clock time, psychological time and spiritual time. Nature's time is defined by the natural movement and changing of the seasons. A relentless cyclical process that is neither fast nor slow. It just is, has always been and will likely forever be. Aligning our self with the rhythm of the cycles of the natural world is therapeutic for a human being. The act of slowing the activity within our consciousness in order to give our attention to fully see and be with the natural world 'out there' cultivates a deeper awareness of our own inner world.

Lie on a grassy bank on a summer evening and stare up at the night sky and it's almost impossible not to allow your consciousness, which is you, to move into a silent, profound, unlimited spaciousness. In such moments our life feels very different. It can be humbling and yet exhilarating, at almost the same 'time'. But it's something we tend to do less and less as more of us become increasingly obsessed with our relationship to our slick and sophisticated machines and all that they can seemingly 'do' for us.

Time Starvation

In some parts of the world there is food famine. In other parts of the world there seems to be a 'time famine'. People actually believe there is a shortage of time. They keep saying, "I don't have enough time... or I have too much to do... or I'm just too busy right now". While no one has ever died due to a shortage of time some may have killed themselves with the anxiety they create due to the belief that there isn't going to be enough ...time! In such moments they have disconnected from natures rhythms. They are trapped in 'clock time' and living a clock driven life. They are likely to be addicted to 'event stimulation'.

Going with the Flow

'Time famine' tends to be a frequent perception in the lifestyle of people in so-called 'developed' countries where 'speed' is worshipped as a modern God. That's probably why by far the most popular workshop/course/seminar in those countries is... yes, you guessed, Time Management! But few realize that 'time management' is an oxymoron. Time is not a commodity like money or rice that can be managed. Although we may speak about the 'flow of time', unlike a river it cannot be blocked, drained or diverted. It's only when you realize you are the creator of time, and that it has its origins in your perceptions, that you become aware of your capacity to shrink or stretch time.

'Time pressure' comes when you decide there is too much to do in an allotted amount of clock time. So you generate anxiety. As soon as you admit and accept that all the things you want to do cannot be done in the allocated clock time your perception changes and the pressure (anxiety) is gone. But that's not easy in an accelerated world of deadlines and pre-planned process timelines. You can never fully anticipate the uncontrollable, the unexpected and the unavoidable along the way.

Often the mistake of living by the clock is compounded by our 'learned neediness'. It's when you make your self-esteem dependent on getting the job done by a certain 'clock time' or when your neediness makes you want the approval of others by meeting their 'clock time deadline' It's your dependence and neediness that generates your 'feelings' of time pressure. As soon as you show any fear of loss of job or loss of approval to those who give you any deadline driven task, that's when 'they' start to use that to motivate you. You then become an adrenaline addict as you create and use the fear of failure and loss to motivate your self.

Do you ever leave anything until the last clock minute? Do you do things quickly to please others? Then you are likely to be an adrenaline addict. Some so-called 'professional people' use this powerful self-manufactured drug during their entire life. Then they wonder why relaxation was so hard and happiness so elusive!

Measuring Space

Clock time is what we use to measure or estimate our experience of the space between then and now and ...then! In reality you cannot measure or manage time itself because it does not exist in any 'form' that can be managed or measured. Time has no independent existence, as most philosophers through the ages have tried to tell us. Everything that we perceive happening 'in time' is happening in our consciousness. Which means time is consciousness. Which means you truly are a 'Time Lord'!

This makes sense when you notice that we each see and sense time passing differently. We all know people for whom time seems to pass oh so slowly. They are serene and deliberate, do one thing at a time, and just seem, well, slow and unhurried about everything. Others are speedy, always rushing, always speeding and doing everything fast, trying to do too many things at once to such an extent we wonder what they are taking!

They both live in the same outer world but time is passing differently in their inner world, in their psychological universe. Both are creating their 'time' differently. This is why time is our personal creation. Confirmed by the simple fact that when you make your self 'unconscious' every night when you go to bed, time completely disappears!

Time and Space Management!

This is also why time management is really self-management in the deepest and truest sense. Most time management seminars could really be renamed "How to be more Organized and Efficient". They are more about how to create and handle events efficiently in the clock driven world 'out there'.

Managing 'real time' would then be about how you create your personal sense of time within your own consciousness. That's where you may apply a simple formula. If you want to 'stretch time' then think less. Why? Because thoughts are the events you create within your own consciousness. The more you think the faster time will seem to pass. Time will seem to shrink! Think less and become more aware of the space between your thoughts (your inner events) and you will get the sense of time slowing down and expanding.

Insperienced meditators have known this for several thousand years. Hence the efficacy of practices such as meditation and contemplation, in which you slow thoughts down, thus creating more space between thoughts. It's in this space that we see more clearly (without thinking about what we are seeing!) and feel more deeply (before thinking about what we feel!).

What do we feel? A profound sense of meaningfulness, of significance, of completeness, of serene contentment, of quiet joyfulness, of unbounded acceptance and appreciation for everyone and everything. It's different for different people. It depends how deeply you enter your own inner space. But these are some of the ingredients that make up the very juice of life itself.

It seems more of us now find it harder to create and taste this juice as we become distracted and addicted to the stimulation of outer events and our relationships (which are just more events) in the world. There does seem to be some juice in such events/relationships that come from 'outside in' but they bring little 'nourishment' if we use them just for personal stimulation.

And finally to spiritual time! Take a moment to imagine you have gone beyond the awareness of all outer events ...for a few clock minutes! Including the sounds of the ticking clock! Imagine you were able to stay in the inner space prior to thoughts and feelings, prior to memories and all subconscious impulses. You are now living in the inner space prior to all inner events.

In such an inner state there would be no perception of change or of any space between events. In such moments you have consciously stopped creating time.

You would, in such a moment, be aware of your own timelessness.

But the moment you started to think about it, you wouldn't!

That's why spiritual time, in the purest sense, isn't!

Some call it the 'awareness of your own eternity'!

But that's also another seminar!

BEAUTY

BEYOND BELIEF

Mirror oh mirror
Still on the wall
Is that really me
Why am I so small

Surely not me
Forcing that grin
Do I really possess
Such a sizable chin

And did I just see
Three horrible pimples
Or was it the light
From the lampshades dimples

I need to look good
For others you see
Or I might not be loved
Then I just won't be me

So on with the lotions
Mascaras and foundations
Those eyebrows need trimming
Those nails a cremation!

It's not just the girls
Boys are also acquiring
New hairstyles and eyebrows
Their own beauty aspiring

Now where's my new diet
We're slimming again
The pounds come and go
But too many remain

But deep down inside
Underneath my sanity
Are the weeds of my misery
Growing out of my vanity

You have likely absorbed the belief that it's a blessing to look beautiful.

But, for many, it's more often a curse.

Are you using your belief that you are beautiful to sabotage your intelligence? That's often, not always, what beautiful looking people do. But they often don't know what to do about it until it's too late.

That physical beauty can be a curse is not an easy thing for beautiful people to recognize. It can be even harder to understand. It's not bad to look fabulous, just unfortunate, for some!

Almost all of us grow up believing I am what I look like. This can be the seed for much misery to come. Especially those who either learn to believe they are drop dead stunningly gorgeous or those who aspire to be so.

From a young age beautiful people tend to become dependent on others to affirm how beautiful they look. With compliments flowing frequently to acknowledge that he or she is a 'looker' they learn to acquire the approval of others based on appearance. They then mistake attention for approval and mistake approval for love. It frequently becomes like any other addiction, hard to kick.

If their physical beauty isn't consistently affirmed by others they will make themselves miserable and insecure. As a result it often follows that they will not develop their natural intelligence. For many of 'the beautiful people', but not all, as time goes on the 'curse' of believing 'I am beautiful' becomes hard to shake off.

As soon as your physical appearance starts receiving the enthusiastic attention of others, unless you are very aware, you will start strengthening your sense of self, your identity, around how you look in the mirror. This leads to a craving for others acknowledgement and recognition. Self worth is then defined by 'how good you look', which generates a deepening neediness for attention, approval and affirmation.

Over time, often the teenage years, this can lead to a lazy intellect. There is less incentive to develop ones intellectual capacity and the consequent intelligence. When ones appearance translates into opportunities to walk through certain doors, and privilege is granted, a superficial life becomes an easy life. The main work required is time spent in front of the mirror before heading out to face the world each day.

Cashing in on physical beauty may seem like the creative, resourceful and intelligent thing to do. But if it results in a dependency on the glances and smiles, invitations and income, that arrive frequently from others, the belief that 'I am so beautiful' becomes a trap. Exploitation and usury will likely be waiting on many corners. If a subtle laziness of intellect kicks in, alongside an obsession with appearance and the need to please, it can become harder to cope with life's inevitable challenges. Both wisdom and strength of character are underdeveloped.

For many people with great physical beauty 'authentic beauty' is never cultivated. This is the beauty that is not seen in the mirror or found on the surface, but has its roots in character. This is the beauty that comes from inside out. Some call it goodness. Many call it virtue. This is the beauty that touches others at the heart of their being and does not arouse desire within the heart of their body!

We all possess such 'beauty'. But if we are physically beautiful, if we are born with a set of genes that makes our appearance attractive to others, we can all too happily allow that to be the shaper of our destiny without ever knowing there is a deeper level of beauty to be discovered.

It's not so easy to develop a beautiful character when the desire to be seen as physically beautiful has been planted and nurtured from a young age. So how can you make the transition and shift the emphasis from what is seen in the mirror in the bathroom to what is seen in the mirror of ones own and others hearts?

One way is to think of someone you know who is not at all good looking. They don't seek the attentions and approval of others at that level. At the same time they are warmly held in the highest regard by others. Not for how they look, but for their personality, their character, and the benevolent intentions they bring to their relationships.

Profile the virtues of this person. Illustrate their character. Identify the intangible attributes that they bring to the party, so to speak, that makes them warmly appreciated as a person by all. Once you have that picture don't try to be it. Don't try to imitate it. Just explore each characteristic as if you already have your own version of it. As you do you'll start to notice what's in the way of your own inner beauty.

You will notice behaviors and intentions that are distorting the quality of your character. You'll notice habits and tendencies that are sabotaging the beauty of your being. Sit with them and you will start to see the beliefs you have learned that are the root cause of any absence of 'beauty of character'.

Don't beat your self up when you notice how difficult it seems to bring your kindness, your acceptance of others, your compassion, your caring, to the actual interactive party called life. Play with the profile of a beautiful character with a quiet curiosity, without any self-judgment. Keep noticing and those characteristics will start to show up in your own actions and interactions.

In small ways at first. But they will appear.

They are all already there within you. As they emerge you will start to know your own beauty, your true beauty. As you do you will be less and less needy of the attention, affirmation and approval of others.

Your natural intelligence will flourish.

EMOTION

BEYOND BELIEF

Well what do you know!
Confusion abounds
Around emotions and feelings
There are so many sounds

There's so many opinions
And so many choices
Who would you believe
In this cacophony of voices

Some say that emotions
Come from inside out
Others perceive this
With buckets of doubt

We all know that emotion
Is a disturbance within
Shaping words and actions
Because we can't keep it in

Feeling's a verb
Something you do
While emotion's a noun
You allow to do you!

Love's just an emotion
And happiness the same
Say the voices of reason
Playing the 'intelligence' games

So many myths
About emotions we make
But they all disappear
When you master your state

When you 'feel' loving and joyous
They're not more emotions
When you're truly contented
There's no mental commotion

Do you carry the beliefs that emotion is natural, that you have to fill your endeavors with emotion, that there is something wrong with you if you don't show emotion and that love is just another emotion.

It's all lies!

In media interviews, in movie scripts, in our cappuccino conversations, we often hear the question, "How do/did you feel". But it's a question that usually means WHAT did you feel? HOW do you feel is a separate issue. We all learn HOW to spell, HOW to wash dishes, HOW to drive a car, etc., but it seems very few of us learn HOW to FEEL! In fact it could be argued that no one learns HOW to feel i.e. how to consciously choose your feelings, because no one teaches us! Could that be because so few really know?

Then there is another question, which sits between the WHAT and the HOW of feeling. It's WHY do you feel what you feel! Once again, it seems few people, when asked these questions, can clearly see *the what, why and how* of the one ability we all share as human beings, the ability 'to feel'. Complicating things even further is what we call emotion! When we 'feel emotional' what are emotions exactly, and why are we... feeling them?

There appears to be two reasons why most of us don't really know 'what' we are feeling, most of the time! The first can be found in our education and the second in our body!

An Absence in our Education

The missing ingredients in our formal education were self-understanding and emotional awareness. There was no focus on understanding what we were feeling and why we felt what we felt. Certainly there was no separation between our emotions and feelings. This meant we didn't talk much about the inner world of our self. We didn't discuss our feelings...much! Perhaps we talked occasionally about extreme emotions like excitement or sorrow, but we said little about the more subtle and frequent emotions in between.

That meant we didn't fully develop a language to describe what was going on within our consciousness, where all the emotions that we feel originate, accumulate or repeat. Perhaps the compulsory second language we could encourage future generations to learn would be the Language of Emotion.

The Effects IN Our Body

Which brings us to the second reason why we don't really know what we are feeling. We don't generally register our emotions until they have some 'effect' in our body. We don't notice how they originate within our consciousness and not in our form. We often don't notice the emotional disturbance called worry until it has an effect in our stomach. We don't notice the emotional disturbance called fear until our heart starts racing. We don't notice our angers until our fists clench and our face is hot! By the time we notice these emotions they often just feel 'physical'. So we fail to notice the origins of our emotions in our own minds.

Without a Language

When we **don't** fully develop a language, based on our description of the emotions that we feel, we don't develop 'shared meaning'. That's why most conversations around understanding emotions don't go very far, don't last very long and often regress either into an argument or the glazed look of boredom!

We don't start with, "Well what do you mean exactly when you say 'emotion'?" And very often, when we do ask the question, 'what do you feel about that', we really mean what do you 'think' about that! We don't realize we really mean 'thought'. Then we become confused and emotional, and end up wondering why we are feeling so ...agitated!

So, for many of us, emotions, feelings and thoughts become brilliantly entangled. From this entanglement arises so many beliefs about our emotions that are misleading at best and fatal at worst.

Read ten different writers, who sometimes call themselves 'experts' on the subject of emotion/feelings, and you will likely find ten different perspectives and perceptions. It all adds up to a fogginess about WHAT we are feeling, which stops us seeing WHY we are feeling what we feel. And we need to see WHY if we are to know and understand HOW to feel and be the master of our feelings ...again!

An Unresolvable Catch 22

That said, it's fairly obvious to most of us that we now live in a highly 'emotional' world. It seems many people live in an emotional state most of the time. All they are feeling are their emotions ...most of the time! And when they're not, they want to!

This diminishes our clarity around 'the what' and 'the how' of our feelings. Why, because in order to clearly see and understand the WHY and the HOW of feeling we need to be free of emotion! When you are angry you cannot see the cause of the anger is ...in you! When you are sad and fearful you can't see the cause of your sadness and fear is ...in you! So you won't be able to see exactly WHY you made yourself angry or sad or fearful as long as you are in those emotional states!

Therein lies the ultimate Catch 22. It also explains why the practice of meditation becomes so useful. One of the results of 'meditation practice' is the ability to untangle ones 'self' from all emotional disturbance in order to restore mastery of your feelings!

I cover all of this in the book BEING Your Self. Suffice to say emotions are felt, but not all feelings are emotions. Emotions arise from the ego and are signs we are sabotaging our wellbeing. Yet emotions are addictive, as well as exhausting. Love is not an emotion. To understand your emotions and how you create them requires insight into your own consciousness to 'see' where and how the emotion is created.

Hence the cultivation of emotional intelligence is not really possible until there is a certain level of 'spiritual intelligence'. That means a deeper awareness of how your consciousness, which is you, the spiritual being that you are, actually works.

Once you start to see with greater clarity what and how you are creating your emotions you will notice that:

- When you are truly loving you are not emotional.

- When you are emotional you are lost in the emotion.

- When you are emotional you cannot choose your feelings.

- When you are emotional the cause is some level of attachment.

- When you are emotional your mind will also be at it's busiest.

- When you are emotional you are not relaxed at any level.

- When you are emotional you are not intelligent.

- When you are emotional you are a slave to the world around you or your imagination of the world around you.

- When you are emotional you are mostly busy with your own emotions and therefore less available for others.

- When you are emotional you are misusing and often exhausting your own energy.

- When you create certain emotions you are likely to mistakenly believe this is how to feel alive.

- When you are emotional you are not a free being.

When was the last time you were emotional?   Why did you emote? What was the effect on your thinking and decision making?

Only self-enquiry can help you to see the how, what and why of your own emotions.   Only then can you cultivate the clarity that allows you to be beyond all those beliefs about emotion that keep you trapped in emotional addiction and emotional exhaustion.

Are you ready to gather some 'intel'?

The next time you notice you became emotional about anything take five minutes once the emotion has passed and sit quietly with the questions:

1 - what emotion did I create? (develops the language)

2 - why did I create that emotion? (develops the understanding)

PROBLEMS

BEYOND BELIEF

Problems problems everywhere
And not a moment to think
I just can't face them anymore
Time for another drink!

It's always just so easy
To see things with that dread
Always what's going wrong
Is the first thing to be said

If you stop and look within
There's a good chance you will see
The problem's not out there
It's always made 'in me'

It's a question of perception
It's the world that you create
With your thoughts and then your feelings
According to your state

When you're feeling grey and down
There's more problems every day
But when you're light and sunny
They all seem to fade away

To free yourself of such difficulty
Change the way that you perceive
Start seeing what's seems so wrong
As opportunities you receive

Yes it's entirely up to you
To see things in brighter ways
To choose the way you live your life
And manufacture happier days

Look at that glass again
Half empty or half full
You know the way to see it
To relax and just be cool

There seems to be those who have decided life is one great list of problems to be suffered and struggled with.

But you believe differently, yes?

Whether you speak French, Russian, Italian or Croatian it seems that many of us share a common language. It's called 'Problemian'! It's a language that is built around believing, perceiving, thinking and talking in terms of 'the problem'. It sounds like, "There's a problem with... I have a major problem... You know what I think the problem is... This thing is a problem... The problem with you is..."!

It's a linguistic trap, a habitual interpretation, a perceptual enclave, and it happens when you 'see' people, situations and events as ... a problem! Whenever I fall into one of these traps I notice I am just being lazy!

The belief that 'there is a problem' also keeps you searching for solutions. It's a search that also becomes a habit. It keeps you in a state of subtle tension between here (the problem) and there (the solution).

Some people become so 'problem centric' that when there obviously aren't any problems they become uncomfortable and start consciously and unconsciously looking for them! Others will even fabricate a problem so they can go hunting for a solution! It gives them a sense of purpose. And occasionally you get an invitation to the seminar that will solve all your problems entitled 'The Problem of Positive Thinking'!

When you decide there's a problem we make that decision within your own consciousness. In truth that's where the problem is created (as a problem) and where it exists (as a problem). It is simply a perception, an interpretation. That's not to say that the situation on the ground out there doesn't exist. But it's just a situation. It's neither problematic or not problematic, until you decide either way for our self.

Problems tend to be personal perceptions and interpretations of adversity that we then use to generate some emotional suffering, however minimal! If you can kick the habit of perceiving and framing things/people/events as problems you may notice that situations are just situations and conditions that can be described by facts. In other words, without making your self unhappy.

A million starving people can be a BIG problem or simply a fact that invites us to respond to do what we can to alleviate the condition/situation. When we see it as a BIG problem we create an emotional heaviness about the situation. Maybe even anger as we seek someone to blame, thereby draining our energy. But if you can stand back and see without emotion, you will be able to create greater clarity about what needs to be done. Then you have the choice to act, or not, as the case may be.

That's the easy dissolution of a problem i.e. by changing your perception/interpretation of what you see. An example that is perhaps a little more challenging and a little closer to home might be your dire personal financial situation. You could continue residing in your dark 'this is bad' perception. Thinking this is a BIG problem, and allowing it to weigh heavily on your consciousness. Or you can decide to re-interpret it as:

a) a message to be less dependent on monetary wealth for your feelings of security/happiness or

b) to check your mindset around money and see if you are sabotaging your ability to attract/earn monetary energy or

c) a challenge to be more creatively resourceful and start generating alternative streams of income or ...all three!

To do this it is necessary to re-interpret your financial situation and cease to 'see it' as a big problem that requires some magic bullet, some awesome solution, or someone to blame. It is simply a state of affairs right now that can be used as an opportunity to learn about ones self in the process of improving the situation.

It's Them!

Then of course there is the perception of 'them'. They're the problem! "Can't get on with 'them'. Don't even want to speak to 'them'. It's 'them' that's making me feel angry/upset/sad/unhappy. It's 'them' that's in the way".

Many people live their entire lives projecting their perceptions and emotions on to others. And they don't even notice they are doing it. Some however do awaken to a deeper truth that reminds them that the 'other person is never the problem'. C'est moi! C'est always moi!

Only when we realize that it's not 'them' that creates our feelings is it possible to see the real cause of our emotional state. It is profoundly simple! In all instances where we believe it's them that's the problem, it's not! It's our expectation of them that is not being fulfilled that is shaping our perception to see them as 'the problem'. Which just means we are still making 'them' responsible for our wellbeing.

Only when we fully realize that our happiness, contentment, satisfaction, joy, is an 'inside job' will all our problems start to disappear. (see chapter on Happiness).

There are no problems just people doing what they are doing, just situations coming into view and then fading from view, just a world around us that is constantly changing. Yes there is much violence. There is much abuse. There is much conflict. But if we react emotionally we are just adding our violence to the sum total of violence in the world.

We are often surrounded by people who still 'believe' they have problems. They are therefore quick to energize their perceptual habit of problem spotting. It seems easier to join in. Don't. It only encourages them to continue disempowering themselves.

In reality, there are no problems, if you so decide! When you see the world the way it really is, you realize it is just the way it is. This is not a way of avoiding engaging and dealing with other people and life around you. It's a mindset that frees you from the habit of creating a perception of what you want to 'believe' is in the way. Realizing this helps you break the lazy habit of looking for what's always wrong, and realizing that there is nothing in the way, and ultimately nothing is going wrong.

Everything is just 'going'. Everything can always be improved, for sure. But you won't be able to see and create improvement if you are blinding and paralyzing your self with a perception that says, "Oh God, this is a big problem".

This is not an easy perspective to grasp after a lifetime of being programmed to perceive 'the problem' and learning the language of problemian! Try living a complete day without perceiving, interpreting, framing anything or anyone as 'a problem'. You'll first notice how strong the habit is, how that mindset wants to take over.

But if you hang in there you will likely notice a feeling of lightness, followed by feeling of contentment, along with the feeling of having a renewed power over your mental creation.

All are signs that your perception is no longer being overpowered and shaped by the perceptions and interpretation of others. Interpretations that are often delivered so efficiently to your mental doorstep by the media.

Perhaps you will end the day with the thought, "I truly was the master of my life today. Nothing got to me. I didn't pull my self down".

Or, if you want to revert to the most common switch of perception, somewhat clichéd now, but still valid, say to your self, "There are no problems, only opportunities".

Then you only ever need to ask one question in various ways.

What opportunities came my way today? Why, for me, was this situation, this event, this person, an opportunity and not a ...?

INTELLIGENCE

BEYOND BELIEF

So what did you learn
Every day in that classroom
What can you remember
There's a test coming soon!

You studied so hard
Late nights, bleary eyes
Just to remember
How to cross T's and dot I's

But now you know better
It just wasn't learning
Just a test of your memory
So you could start earning

It's the great deception
To keep you in line
Convinced that your grades
Would make everything fine

But reality dawns
Something was missing
No subject called life
No lessons for living

Once out in the world
It's all about connection
How to relate
And the meaning of affection

Life skills are the key
To getting along
But they don't come in a book
Nor the words of a song

That's why learning begins
When you step into the day
Engaging with real people
In intelligent ways

That's when you'll know
What's exactly amiss
From your own repertoire
Much more than a kiss

Most of us learn to believe that learning happens by listening and memorizing, and that intelligence follows.

Who were 'they' kidding!

You may have had a good education but did you really learn anything?

What is the difference between *education* and *learning*?

An *education* is something you acquire in an institution whereas *learning* is a continuous dynamic in a process called life.

Unfortunately most of us learned to confuse one with the other when 'they' taught us that learning was memorizing and life was a stroll in the park. As soon as we finished with school, college or university many of us could be heard rejoicing with the words, "Thank goodness that learning stuff is over, now I can go and make some money"! Little did we realize our learning had just begun.

What's the difference between *education* and *intelligence*?

Education is based on receiving, holding and processing information towards some standard of 'academic' success. Whereas *intelligence* is based on awareness, understanding and the creation of one's thoughts and feelings, perceptions and attitudes, in the process of building relationships along with making and taking decisions and actions.

Once again we are confused when we believe our academic qualifications are a route to self-improvement. They are merely a measure of our memory at a particular point in time, often within a narrow specialist area. They are not a sign of how well we know ourselves, or how well we are able to manage our thoughts and feelings or build loving relationships with others.

What's the difference between *learning* and *intelligence*?

Learning is something you do, whereas *intelligence* is something you already have and cultivate as you experience life. Our confusion of one with the other means we 'believe' we are becoming more intelligent when we believe we are learning through our formal education, which is essentially memorizing and processing. The reverse is truer i.e. it requires intelligence to realize that the main way to increase our intelligence is to unlearn many of the beliefs we are taught to remember in our formal education.

Rational Intelligence

The basic level of intelligence we use in our formal education is easy to develop. It is still the most common route to our decisions. Known as 'rational intelligence' it tends to be a mechanical and sequential process within our consciousness in which we use reason, logic and analysis, while drawing on past experience, to make decisions, choices and take action.

It takes time, requires much 'thinking', and easily drains our mental energy. Rational intelligence has its deepest roots in a material self-perception. When we see ourselves only as material beings, finite and limited, the physical world is perceived as the primary reality - mechanical, predictable and controllable. What we see around us becomes either threatening or pleasurable.

On the one hand we learn that the world is something that is to be survived. While on the other hand we believe it is a source of sensual stimulation and therefore happiness. For these 'reasons' we see it as something we need to control, order and exploit. This in turn drives the development of our rational skills as we seek to understand how the world works and create physical and mechanical (rational) ways to control and exploit our environment.

To cut a long story extremely short the outcome is the 'materialist paradigm' of which the most recent manifestation is globalization. This is facilitated and characterized by technology and the capacity to connect and communicate across vast distances at lightening speeds.

But this 'interconnection' is at the most superficial level, that of information. The paradox is while it appears to signal progress by making the world smaller and more interconnected, technology tends to isolate more than unify, as we each focus mostly on our personal keyboards and screens!

Rationality still rules the world. But the result seems to be reflected in the magnitude and quantity of stress, conflict and violence, which have never been so varied and widespread. We have used our rational intelligence to create brilliant technologies, fast. By doing so we have shrunk the world, bringing every living being on the planet physically closer together than at anytime in human history.

The reality however, is that in our hearts we have never been further apart. While we may speak to each other more, we actually say less. While we exchange massive amounts of information, we share, develop and apply less wisdom.

A world built by scientific research and technological development may be an impressive creation of our rational intelligence and skills. But it can appear to be an increasingly unhappy world, rapidly being stripped of the human feelings of caring, empathy and compassion. It is a world that depends more and more on physical stimulation delivered by wifi and screens.

However it seems we are still determined to 'believe' we are making progress.

What do you perceive? Do you think that's true?

Emotional Intelligence

Both the speed of change and the apparent deterioration of the human capacity to form and sustain harmonious relationships have created the need and the context for the cultivation of 'emotional intelligence' (EQ). Now an established topic in the corporate world of leadership/management development, it is also seeping into academic education systems.

Emotional intelligence is the awareness of ones own emotions and feelings and the ability to see and understand their cause. This is the basis of being able to free your self from your emotions i.e. stop creating them, and be the master of your feelings. EQ is the capacity to be sensitive to and empathize with another's emotional state. Often confused with sympathy, empathy is an obvious necessity in relationship building, establishing mutual understanding, conflict resolution and therefore living and working with others.

Would you say you are emotionally intelligent? Do you know what emotions are? Or do you carry some vague beliefs about emotions and feelings?

Rational intelligence has traditionally focused on the 'task'. We learn that going to work means we go to do a job. Emotional intelligence reminds us we can't get the job done effectively and consistently unless we 'get along' with people. The emotionally intelligent individual goes to work to form and build relationships and partnerships as much as getting a job done. It sounds obvious and easy but for many it's not. Nothing in our formal education prepares us.

While IQ (task focus) 'seems' to bring us closer together through technological creativity the resulting isolation often drives us further apart. EQ (relationship focus) can appear to drive us further apart ...at first. In the process of getting to know and understand others, our own resistances and prejudices tend to be triggered and highlighted. But if we can work through those using our emotional intelligence it eventually brings us closer together.

Spiritual Intelligence

The deepest level of intelligence is spiritual intelligence. Based in the awareness of clear sense of 'who I am' as opposed to who I have been taught to believe I am or who I would like to be. It is built on a conscious connection to our original nature, often referred to as the source of our core values.

Spiritual intelligence is the internal capacity to know and live by the true meaning and expression of love. When neither blocked or distorted by attachment or dependency, someone acting from love embraces, encourages and uplifts others. Not an easy task in a world where we are often 'educated' believe in the opposite i.e. compete, discourage and avoid.

Cultivation of your spiritual intelligence requires periods of introversion and introspection, combined with the practices of meditation and contemplation. From this comes a deeper awareness of who and what I am, prior to the beliefs already assimilated about 'me'. In the context of your relationships spiritual intelligence is the capacity to see beyond labels and perceive all others as spiritual beings. When fully developed it is the ultimate unifier.

If your spiritual intelligence is to flourish it is necessary to keep transcending all belief. Belief is not enough. It gets in the way of seeing and realizing what is true and real. This is an insight and awareness that cannot be taught. It requires introspective curiosity exercised along side the practice of meditation. One has to 'see' for one self.

These levels of intelligence already exist within you, within everyone. But they are seldom consciously cultivated. They are also interconnected. It's somewhat false to try to separate them and I do so only for the purpose of description. Only when you cultivate your SQ will you begin to fully understand why and how you make yourself emotional. Only when you cultivate your EQ will you notice how you sabotage your ability to be rational and think clearly and logically.

There are so many beliefs to kill under this heading of 'intelligence'. Not least the one that says you can never be intelligent because you didn't do well in your education.

In many ways it's good news if you have left school. It means you are now enrolled in the BIG school of life itself. It is a school in which every scene is a page in the Book of Life, filled with symbols and laden with meaning. Being able to read the book that is constantly taking shape around you is beyond the boundaries of academia and beyond the capacity of rationality.

That's why the true school is not out there. It is consciousness itself. It is your 'self'. It is within consciousness that you create your own reality. It is there that you create your vision, your decisions, do your learning, generate your feelings, and create the ways in which you will relate to others.

Welcome back to school! A very private, invisible school.

Where you will need to 'unlearn' much, in order to cultivate your intelligence.

REALITY

BEYOND BELIEF

So what is false
And what is real
Why don't you know
How to perceive the real

Until you discover
What is real and true
You will be confused
About all that you do

The primary reality
Is not out there
Like your deepest feelings
It's entirely in 'here'

But seeing and knowing
This reality in you
Requires your stillness
And your silence too

Be quiet and watch
Be aware and you'll be
The one who is watching
The 'real' you will see

That's when you'll know
That reality out there
Is not where you thought
It's always right here

On that fated day
You will come to see
What seems out there
Is really here in me

You may also notice
How everything is one
Existing in you
And you are the sun

Not the sun in the sky
But the one in your heart
As you shine into all
Each day a new start

You are probably under the illusion that the primary 'reality' lies out there in the material world around you.

But this belief is the cause of so much human unhappiness.

See if the following is true for you.

There are three realities in life. The third reality is the world around you 'out there'. It's the world of people, situations and events. A world that is constantly changing over which you have no control.

The secondary reality is the world 'in here', within your own consciousness. This is the world of your thoughts and feelings, your decisions and attitudes. In this world, IF you were fully awake and aware, you would have total control.

Paradoxically, if you really were fully awake and aware, it would not feel like you were controlling anything. Whatever would arise 'in here' in response to the world 'out there' would arise naturally and accurately ...if you were fully awake and aware. Right now there are many moments when you think you have no control over your inner world. Those moments are often called 'emotional reactions'. They are born 'in here'.

Then there is the primary reality which is you, the 'self'. This is the world of pure being. It's you being your self prior to thinking, feeling and experiencing. It's a world that is silent and still, that never changes. It's around this primary reality, which is you, that the second reality spins.

We all tend to be programmed to believe the third reality is the primary reality. We learn to mistake the world around us 'out there' to be the only reality. In that world 'out there', we are told and we believe, that we will find love and happiness, peace and prosperity.

So we go searching for our happiness in that world 'out there', which guarantees we will make our self unhappy. (see Happiness) Pleasure can be found when we use the world around us to stimulate our senses. But pleasure is not happiness. Pleasure gives us sensual highs, inevitably followed by lows. Hence the instability that comes from believing reality is only 'out there'.

You can study and know the third reality. That's called science. You can study and know the secondary reality. That's called psychology. But you cannot study the primary reality of your own being. And there is nothing to know! But it's real. It is the primary reality for us all. Have you 'insperienced' it yet?

Scientific knowledge is based on information created from observation and physical measurements. Psychological knowledge is gathered from listening to people describe their thoughts and feelings and observing their behaviors. Both scientific and psychological fields of endeavor, studying the second and third realities, attempt to reach beyond just believing. They seek the kind of evidence that allows them to say 'we now know'. But there are no certainties in either of those realities.

Knowledge of being, the primary reality, as in gathering information about being, is impossible. You can only know that you, the being, at your core, are silent and still. You can know your self as love. But when you are silent and in a loving state there is no need to 'know' it and you certainly would not be 'thinking it'!

Ultimately knowledge of 'being' is unnecessary to living this life. But knowing and understanding how you create your thoughts and feelings, perceptions and intentions, which populate your secondary reality, is extremely helpful. Some would say essential, to living this life.

But that is almost impossible to see clearly until you realize fully that the world 'out there' is not the primary reality.

Those worlds are there. They are not illusions. They are real. But as long as we mistakenly attribute primacy to either we will be deluded and, as a result, suffer. So that leaves us with a big question. How do we restore the awareness of the correct order of reality, which is now the wrong way round and upside down? This takes us into the subject of what is commonly termed 'spirituality'.

Another way to ask this question is how do I know I am the spiritual being at the center of everything that I experience and insperience? How do I know I am essentially still and silent at the core of my being? How do I know that 'I' do not have the same characteristics as the stuff that makes up the material world starting with the body I occupy?

Now we are back in the territory of the mystic. The mystic is a practising meditator. To the mystic, meditation is not a technique. It's an awareness. It's being aware of the right order of reality and then allowing that awareness to inform the heart and the mind as he or she interacts with the world.

Let's imagine you are learning to be a mystic. You are learning to become more aware. You would start by practising self-awareness. That means practising being aware there is a you, an I, an existing being, as distinct from your thoughts and feelings. This practise eventually induces the realization you are awareness itself.

You start to notice that while the world seems to be 'out there' in time and space, it is also 'in here', within you. You would notice that it's you who decides what and who to create and sustain 'in here' within you. You would notice you were doing that in your mind as you 'receive' the world.

You would notice, with the on going practice of awareness, that it's you that decides what to allow to 'be in' your consciousness as you create your 'version' of out there in here ...so to speak. You are the creator of your version of whomever and whatever you decide to perceive, 'in here'.

You also notice how you distort your own creation with your personal judgments, comparisons and criticisms, which arise from your beliefs. The more you notice this, the less you do it. If for no other reason than you sense you would like to create your reality with no distortions at all.

With your increasing awareness you can see how you can quietly end all your old habits of filtering in judgmental and critical ways. You become able to create and hold the world with a pure vision, untainted and undistorted by any belief.

That's the moment you realize that it's you, not your thoughts or feelings, that gives existence to the world within you. You notice there are moments when you exist without thinking or feeling anything. You are existence itself. And it's you that is 'giving existence' to everything, in you.

You can probably appreciate it's almost impossible to describe these levels of awareness in words. So it's a huge mistake to convert them into just another set of beliefs.

One of the purest 'insperiences' of the mystic is this realization that 'I am the master creator'. Not in an egotistical sense but in a natural state of humility. Both the capacity to be this, and the awareness of this, disappears whenever the ego appears.

The mystic is clearly aware that yes there is a self, a me, an 'I'. But in it's purest form, in 'your' purest form, you don't 'think it'. There is no need. Purest form of consciousness just means you are in your utterly naked inner state. When you are naked all the ways of 'creating an identity', in other words creating an ego, have ended. You can see that what you used to construct your ego were just passing ideas, memories, images, beliefs, and therefore not the REAL you.

In the naked state you no longer need or have the urge to add anything to you, no need to embellish anything in your life, no desire to be anyone in the world, or want anything from the world. You are fully aware that you are in the world but not of the world. In this naked state you are naturally in a state of contentment. This contentedness is your authentic happiness.

This is of course the destiny of someone who has become progressively enlightened. Words can only describe, point at, what it's like to be there. They are somewhat inadequate to describe the journey and the destination itself.

We are all mystics for we are all the same at the heart of our being. We are all awareness itself. We are all existence itself. But as soon as we animate form, as soon as we begin to flower into conscious existence in this material reality, as soon as we begin to act and interact, we start to create our own unique story.

Our life, our creative process, becomes unique.

The seed that was the silent self, the still self, begins to germinate and grow.

From that moment onwards reality gradually and naturally fragments as we bring the gifts of joy out of our heart, and love into the world, in an infinite number of ways.

And that's OK. It is as it should be. But that fragmentation increases. Over many centuries it picks up pace. Hence the world that we see today is now severely fragmented at 'all levels'.

Until one day, it's that time, once again.

To be still and know you are simply the 'I' that says 'I am'.

CONCLUSIONS

BEYOND BELIEF

Regardless of where we are
We all share one illusion
There are endings to be faced
There is always a conclusion

Yet you already know
That all things must go on
Life and living never stop
Nothing's short and nothing's long

But the way we speak and live
It's as if we want things done
As we move on to the next task
Running here and there's no fun

Jobs completed, cups are won
Each seems to spell the end
Of yet one more endeavor
Until it's time to start again

But it all becomes so obvious
As on and on we go
Nothing real is ever final
The game of life just flows

When it's fully realized
There are no endings or full stops
A new serenity arises
As we forget about the clock

It's all cyclical you see
The day the year the seasons
Inviting us to live
Beyond the boundaries of reason

Thoughts seem to have their end point
All that noise just can't go on
But the intuitions of the heart
Are like a never ending song

**You have been conditioned to believe
'all things come to an end'.
But do they really?**

It's highly unlikely. Here's why.

Have you ever noticed a tendency to rush towards conclusion? It can easily become one of our deepest habits, based in the belief that there are endings to stories, processes, journeys, relationships and even our life. It's the belief that there must be a last moment, a final scene, a dramatic, climactic crescendo, then a descent into a vacuous silence that signals.... the end!

But it's an illusion. Yes of course the movie ends and the credits roll. But the movie is not real. It's just continuously moving colored lights projected on to a screen. It's just dancing images that we filter through our perception and ascribe our personal meaning. After the lights stop flickering on the screen, the movie continues in the place where the movie was really created and seen, within our consciousness. We continue.

The movie that is 'real life' goes on never-endingly. We allow it to go on, but only when we realize it's just a movie! Most of the time we are looking forward to the end of, well ...something.

The ending of a relationship seems to be the end of 'the relationship', but it isn't. It can never end. We may never physically see and meet that person ever again, but the relationship abides within our consciousness, sometimes consciously, sometimes subconsciously, as a living memory. And memories are forever! That's why wars seem to end when the battlefield is empty, and the peace treaty is signed. But they don't end while they rage on in the minds and hearts of men.

Arrival in London from Paris, or in Beirut from Seoul, may appear to be a journeys end, but in reality it's not, because the destination is not a place where we sit and then suddenly do nothing. They are not 'end points' in our life. Thought and action doesn't end when we physically arrive somewhere. And besides, what exactly is 'where'?

London and Paris are not even places, just labels for pieces of land and buildings. Where do London and Paris, or any city for that matter, begin and end? Is there a line drawn in a field somewhere? No, they are just ideas which become agreed labels for geographical locations where people congregate. Locations where everything and everyone is perpetually moving, changing, shifting ... without end.

What really pulls the rug out from under the 'illusion of conclusion' are the many cycles which exist around us in the world we share. The water cycle, the carbon cycle, the economic cycle, the night and day cycle and the cycle of the seasons. They are all never ending. Perpetual in their motion and there to remind us everyday that in any cycle there are no conclusions.

Even our own personal life cycle has not been proved to have a conclusion. At the point of what is called death, the material of the body continues on as it reverts to its five constituent elements and becomes food! And no one has yet demonstrated exactly what happens to consciousness when it decides to exit the temple of form.

Does anyone know the beginning of life, of time? Does anyone know of the ending? It appears not. There are many theories sustaining many possibilities, but there is nothing conclusive. There can't be because there 'probably isn't'. And implicit in all 'probability' is inconclusiveness ...if you see what I mean! So you could say there are no 'points of beginning' and no ending points. Or if you insist on beginnings and endings then every point, every moment, could be viewed as an ending AND as a beginning, thereby cancelling each other out and creating perpetual continuity.

So why do we develop the tendency to create the illusion of conclusion and want it to come so much we then rush towards it? Why do we often live more focused on endings, on the destination, than on the journey there? Why do we jump to conclusions so quickly only to realize it wasn't a conclusion at all? There are seven possible reasons and, as you will probably notice, each one is ...inconclusive!

We believe in endings *because we want 'it' to be over.*

Whether it is the journey, the relationship or the task, we often want it to finish fast because we do not like the journey, or the person or the process of the task. There is no joy. And the absence of joy means the presence of some level of misery. So we hurry towards the end so we can be free of our misery and move on to something else and the promise of something better.

What we don't realize is the joy we are missing cannot be discovered in the task, or in the relationship, or the journey, only within ourselves. But no one told us that. If we knew that then we might learn to find joy in ourselves regardless of what we are doing, who we are with and wherever we 'appear' to be going. Have you ever noticed that when you really 'enjoy' doing something or being with someone you never look at your watch? Your awareness is in a timeless state and you never invoke the illusion of a conclusion. You forget about endings and arrivals.

We believe in endings *because pleasure must fade*

Yes of course the chocolate bar comes to an end, as does the taste of the chocolate. Or does it? The memory of the taste does not. It is that memory that continues, and sets up the craving for the next bar and what seems to be a new pleasure.

So we seem to have beginnings and endings of frequent pleasures, sustaining the idea that there are 'pleasure endings' over which we have no control. And yet, at a deeper level, we might discover that the real 'pleasure of life' is self generated and not stimulated. But as long as we believe that the pleasures of life are stimulated we are destined to sustain one of our favorite illusions - that all good things must come to an end.

We believe in endings *because we want to avoid understanding the other*

Sometimes when we judge the other there is the tendency to make the judgment final. It's just too inconvenient or too challenging to get to know and understand 'them'. So it's easier to create a conclusion about what they are like and hold that conclusion as a reason to avoid engaging with them. And when someone challenges our judgment, as people do, we also don't want to be proved wrong so we say, "I have made up my mind about him/her, and I have come to the conclusion that...."

In the court room it appears the judge passes a final judgment on the defendant. In reality however they pass a judgment on one aspect of the 'history' of the defendant. All of which appears to conclude the case. But it doesn't. A person is not their history and a person is not 'a case' that can be closed. People's lives go on, and on. Unfortunately we tend to define people by their past history creating an inevitable but false conclusion.

In fact we do the same to ourselves about ourselves. We may even say, or think, "Yes I have always been like this, or behaved like that, it can't be changed, it's the way I am, it's my nature, it's fixed". It provides us with a conclusion that we can then use to justify our avoidance of the effort of changing the ways in which we feel and live.

We believe in endings *because we believe in right and wrong*

Who are we to say what is right and wrong? It certainly varies from culture to culture and it's usually shaped by the prevailing belief systems in that culture. Some say killing animals is wrong and then they eat them. Some say killing people is wrong and then they go to war and kill them. What's right? What is wrong? We tend not to like these kinds of contradictions or ambiguities, and yet we also tend to avoid taking the time to deeply investigate and clarify the morality of our actions. So it's easier to believe in the apparent finality of a right and wrong, especially if we are the creator of that finality.

Some of us have also been taught to equate being happy with being right, so we are always trying to be right so we can be happy. Being right is then seen as an end point, a moment when we can be happy ... at last! So we seek to create and rush towards a finality that might deliver a moment of self-satisfaction. A moment in which we can rest contentedly. But it can only be a moment, and therefore inconclusive, because who has the right to say what is right and what is wrong? Ultimately no one. Is that right? Mmm!

We believe in endings *because we like to tell stories*

The construction of a story usually involves a beginning, middle and an end. The novel or the movie must come to a 'satisfactory conclusion' so that we can go home and get on with our life. But the story is not real, it's manufactured and the idea that there is an ending is also manufactured and built in. The reader of the novel, the watcher of the movie and the actors who play the characters don't suddenly end. 'They' are real and they continue. Real life is a never ending story.

It's as if we believe we can have a moment of rest in a 'neat ending'. But it's really a moment of relief from our own endless personal dramas that we seek. By taking refuge in the happy ending of a fairy tale, or a romantic novel or in the life of the action hero, we learn to believe in the possibility of such 'conclusive moments' in our own life.

ALL stories are therefore 'fairy tales', an escape from the pressure of continuously creating our own life story, which can never have an ending. Or is that just another kind of 'conclusion illusion'?

We believe in endings *because we want to control the process and therefore the outcome*

Victory and triumph are perceived as conclusions to some form of heroic effort. We have a tendency to memorialize the victor and remember them for just one moment, one achievement, one victory. So we learn to aspire, to achieve, to be victorious, to ascend to 'the heights'. Implicit in that aspiration is that when we get there that will be the end of effort, a conclusion to our endeavors. But is it? We still have to get out of bed the next day and face the real challenge if living. That's what makes us all potential heroes – facing the world and living an authentic life without desiring anything to end at any time, in any way.

We believe in endings *because our language is designed to come to a conclusion ...apparently!*

Our construction of language has the idea of endings built in. The linear nature of the sentence must end in a full stop if sense is to be made of what is said. So we create our communication in such a way that there appears to be endings - endings to ideas, to concepts, to experiences, to conversations. But there are no such endings. Everything either continues or fades. But whatever fades still abides somewhere, in some form, usually in consciousness, as memory. And in the meantime the actual creators of language, you and me, we go on and on and on.

And so to conclude, perhaps! One of the greatest paradoxes of our modern lives is we create the illusion of a thousand conclusions, of fixed and final endings, while at the same time we fear 'the end'.

But reality is always there to remind us that what is 'real' goes on. Life flows on. When we fully see and willingly embrace the perpetual never-endingness of all that is real, we enter 'flow'.

Only then can the 'joy of living' dissolve and replace the desire for finality and/or the fear of conclusion.

The End. Not!

CHANGE

BEYOND BELIEF

It appears the world is changing
Triggering suffering and stress
But all is not as it appears
Within your consciousness

That's where you find the space
Round which it all revolves
A silent stillness never changing
Neither diminished or evolved

It's from this quiet subtle space
That everything emerges
Its power profound and limitless
Where all your life converges

It's as if there's no one there
Yet you exist in all your glory
It's from here you will create
Your never-ending story

There is no 'point' within this stillness
Neither meaning nor location
You are not here and neither there
Everywhere is your location

Your stillness is your center
Brought into birth and unto death
As you journey through this world
You sit behind your every breath

It is you, it is I
As if both of us are one
As we 'become' together
There are no shadows in this sun

So take a moment now
To allow your self to be
The unchanging and undying one
You'll be content with all you see

**In the last decade we have witnessed the
re-emergence of some wonderful clichés around change.
Such as, "Be the change you want to see in the world".
Or "When I change the world
changes". And one of the oldest,
"You are what you eat, change your
diet and change your self".**

**But no one questions the beliefs that sit at the
heart of such neat philosophical ideals.**

It's time!

1 Be the change you want to see in the world.

It seems like common sense. It's saying stop pointing outwards and projecting responsibility on to others and waiting for them to change. But why does it seldom make any difference? Why do so few manage to accept complete responsibility? Why do so few manage to 'be the change' they want to see in others?

Could it be that the belief that 'I need to change' gets in the way? Change what? Your thinking? Well OK, changing thinking is not so hard. Just increase your awareness of your thinking, and read and listen to wiser people. Change your behavior? Yes also not so hard for some but almost impossible for others. Habits have taken years to embed within our consciousness and changing them is not going to happen fast. It's too easy to say, "Well what's the point? No one else is changing, so why should I?"

Change your beliefs? Yes you could do that. But then you would start encountering those who don't agree with your beliefs and those who are acting against your beliefs. And there's a lot more of them than there are of you. So what's the point? It would be like trying to swim up the Niagara Falls!

Or maybe it's not about changing you or anything within you. Maybe it's about just returning to your true nature, remembering who you really are, being your true and authentic self. If that is the way then you don't have to change anything. You just have to release all that you are clinging to and then let it all go.

This is of course the aim and the process of the spiritual journey. It's when you realize it's futile to try to change anything in the world out there or even in the world 'in here'. That just puts the energy of your consciousness, that's you, into a state of resistance. And as long as you are in resistance to something or someone, including the past, you will be in conflict. And that's how to make your self unhappy and probably many others around you. That's how most people make themselves unhappy every day.

There's a paradox in all this - if you want to change the world stop trying to change the world. That includes both worlds. The world 'out there' and the world within your consciousness. Just be your self. Be your natural peaceful, loving and happy self. Be that and then whatever thoughts and behaviors arise from your natural state will bring the same gifts to the world. It may not look like you are doing much. Maybe to others you will look like you are lazily doing nothing. But that's the whole point. When you think and act from your natural state, which is always existing within you, you stop trying to interfere with anyone else.

Take a moment, look around the world and notice one of the most popular symptoms of all human unhappiness is people trying to interfere with other people's lives. Resistance takes the form of interference. Take another moment and look within and you will see almost all your dissatisfactions and moments of discontentment are because you are trying to interfere with others lives just in your own mind. I don't mean through action, but just through your thoughts. Are your thoughts regularly going outwards as if to try to fix someone else?

So the practice is not to try to force change in the world or even within you. It is to 'notice' whenever you are trying to do that either with your beliefs, thoughts or actions, and stopping it. The practice is noticing when you are not being your self and trying to be what you are not - a fixer, a complainer, a blamer, a judger, a juror, a jailer - the list is obviously almost endless.

It's likely you want to see the world become a peaceful place where people care about each other and everyone is happy. If so there is no need to 'try to be' the change you want to see in the world. Just realize you 'are' the change you want to see in the world! And so it will be.

Between here and there, now and then, there must be a few turbulent moments along the way. Energies have to be 'resolved'. Situations will inevitable come to test your inner strength. But they also give you the opportunity to reach out and guide others.

But don't wait for others. Are you waiting for 'the other' to change?

2 When I change the world changes.

Well yes and no! It's our old friend perception again. Is the glass half full or half empty? It depends on your perception. What creates your perception? Your beliefs. If you believe the world is dark and dangerous you will start to see darkness and danger. You will then think and act accordingly.

But what is the deepest source of information that will shape your perception? It's not what you believe. That's just something you've learned. It's what you know. And what is the deepest level of knowingness. The level that is beyond belief. It's knowing who you are and knowing what is there within you. Why don't you know 'who you are'? Simply because you have learned to believe you are, or should be, or will be, somebody other than who you really are!

That's why most of our lives are spent striving and struggling to protect who we believe we are. Which is to protect an illusion. What is motivating that? It's the same for us all. We have been taught to believe that we should try 'to be' something other than what we are.

Only when you know your self as you are do you see the world accurately as it is. When you awaken to know yourself as you truly are you begin to know your self as love, as peace, as joy. Once again such words can only 'point' at such states of being. We tend to associate those states of being with acquiring something or someone in the world.

But true love, true joy, true contentment, are feelings that arise totally independent from anything in the world.

With them arises a way of perceiving the world quite different from what we have learned. With this perception you will clearly see those that are still asleep, still unaware of what they are. That vision will be one of understanding and compassion. That compassion will come through your words and actions and there will be an effect on those around you. Where before you judged and resisted now you accept, understand and embrace.

But you didn't change. You just 'restored' your awareness of your true nature, which was always there. It was always 'what' you are.

3 You are what you eat so if you change your diet

you change your self

The belief that you are what you eat is not uncommon especially in the universe of diet conversations and recipe talk. But is that true? Certainly your body is the place where you convert food into bone, muscle and physical energy. But is that you? If you believe so then certainly what you eat is what you become. But if you are not the form you see in the mirror then you are not what you put in your body.

Many people change their diets but it has no effect whatsoever on their perceptions about life, their emotional habits and their behaviors. If it was true that you are what you eat then all we would need to do is change the diet of violent people and they would no longer be violent. But science has not yet found the diet that changes people's memories, thinking and behaving. Why not?

Could it be because you are NOT what you eat? Certainly what you eat may have an effect on your consciousness. The pain of food poisoning will certainly not have you skipping and dancing with joy. The delight at tasting ice cream on a sunny day is a passing effect. It won't be long until there is an argument about who buys the next one.

So the next time you see what is now a somewhat clichéd idea/belief, 'you are what you eat', don't let your inner head nod in acquiescent agreement, question it.

Similarly, that other line 'you are what you think' should perhaps be given the same treatment. Is it true? The answer to this is easier. You create your thoughts but is the creator also the creation? Thoughts come and go, they arise and fade away. But do YOU arise and fade away, in a matter of moments. No! So you are not the thoughts that you create.

To say you are your thoughts is actually a bit of an insult to who you really are! The problem however is we try to be our thoughts. That's exactly how the ego is created. And that's why everyone learns to create an ego.

And that's why there is so much unhappiness in the world.

Go figure... as they say.

OPINION

BEYOND BELIEF

You must have an opinion
That's what so many say
Or you're just another someone
With an empty head all day

It seems only in opining
You've something useful to share
Only then will 'they' listen
Only then will 'they' care

But opinion spells trouble
A fixed belief is at its heart
If it doesn't chime with others
Conflict is bound to start

Then it becomes a habit
To find yourself in a fight
Emotionally wounded
Because you think you're right

You think you can't be happy
Until proved to be accurate
Victorious in all exchanges
Or you just become irate

When your beliefs are challenged
You're rapidly on the offensive
Unless 'they' are louder and clearer
Then it's quickly to the defensive

It's so much simpler to see
No opinion is ever true
Much better to appreciate
So many points of view

Each exchange is then stress free
An open mutual sharing
No more grumpy emotions
A chat that's light and caring

You have probably learned to believe that it's good to have your own opinion on important matters.

But is it?

"But you must have an opinion on the matter," is an exhortation we have probably all heard during some or other conversation. It's seems to imply that if you don't you must be weak, lacking substance and in some way suffering from a deficiency of conviction! Many of us grow up believing that it's essential to have well formed opinions at the ready for those dinner party conversations, serious debates at the bar and even in more intimate moments when you feel the need to 'opine assertively'!

Some people have strong opinions on just about everything for fear of being perceived as intellectually vacant. For others it was their 'parental programming' during childhood that instilled the habit of being opinionated. Some because they want to provoke a reaction, and there are many who genuinely believe they need to have a position, a point of view on ...everything!

Few realize that to have an opinion about anything is almost a cast iron guarantee that suffering must accompany its expression. Why? Well if you have an opinion about having opinions you may find the following somewhat challenging!

The Anatomy of an Opinion!

An opinion is essentially made up of two beliefs. The first belief is about the issue being addressed/explored. The second is usually the *'I am right'* belief, and that may include the *'even if you are also right then I am still more right than you'* belief!

But where does the suffering come from? It's not easy to see but the attachment to ones belief, like the attachment to anything, must generate some fear of loss. The fear usually shows up as some form of mental anxiety. In our heads that anxiety might sound like, "Will they see it the way I see it, will they accept what I say, will they perhaps have a more rounded, deeper, broader, more enlightened belief than me? Will I win the argument?". These are subtle thoughts that tend to flash through our mind before and during the delivery of our opinion. Usually so subtle we often don't notice them! But if we are self aware then we will 'feel' the emotion of anxiety that such thoughts trigger! That's the signal we are making our self ...unhappy!

We all know that old saying, *'you can either be right or you can be happy'*! The highly opinionated personality usually believes happiness is largely derived from being right. They will likely have a tendency towards being somewhat pedantic, interwoven with a need to be affirmed. There are eight reasons why we usually make our self unhappy when we share a 'belief based' opinion. Eight symptoms, the strength of which only you will know according to what you feel within your self at the time.

1 Imposition

When we 'opine' in the presence of others it's as if we are attempting to impose, some would say insinuate, our self upon the other. Any form of imposition will usually invoke a resistance in the other. To which we likely reciprocate with our own resistance. Conflict is not far away, albeit a sometimes gentle, perhaps disguised, interpersonal conflict. This attempt to influence the other will likely require a relationship repair kit ...eventually!

2 Forcing

The emotional content that accompanies the expression of an opinion is usually a tell tale sign of how much we want to win whatever argument is transpiring! Speech is sometimes rushed and the voice becomes raised, which are signs that we are trying to force the other to submit and admit to the rightness of our belief! The longer the other denies us such affirmation the more 'forceful' we will likely become.

3 Controlling

It's hard to notice we are attempting to control the other by trying to get them to see things exactly as we do. We want to control the other's perceptions and perspectives, which of course is impossible. It's an extremely unenlightened way to relate. We may sometimes 'believe' that we have succeeded, especially when 'they' decide to agree with us. But failure is an inevitable destiny of all attempts to 'control' another's perceptions, if only because it's impossible!

4 Narrowed

Holding to one belief is, by definition, to narrow our own perceptions and perspectives. We sabotage our ability to see the bigger picture, to learn from other perspectives, to expand our own horizons. All of which will limit our creativity and our capacity to understand others. To hold on to any belief or belief system is to wear a set of blinkers, one blinker across our mind and the other across our intellect.

5 Disconnected

We all know how much we try to make other people, and the world itself, fit our previously formed beliefs. If you have created a belief that someone was stupid yesterday then you will likely interpret their behavior and ideas as a bit stupid today, regardless of how intelligent they may be. This is what makes us lazy in our relationships. Every time you meet that person you will likely walk away with the feeling that you are not connecting. Why? Because you're not having a relationship with them, but with your belief/s 'about' them. Often referred to as the baggage we bring to a relationship i.e. the beliefs we created yesterday about them are brought to the relationship today.

6 Closed

Attachment to anything means we close our 'self' around the object of attachment. To become closed is to act against our true nature as a human being, which is to be open and free. In the context of opinions we close our self around a belief. We sabotage our own intellectual capacity. The belief becomes the basis for a fixed set of perceptions and thoughts, which then become memories, which are then easily triggered.

That's when, in an interaction with someone, we can be open and freely flowing one minute, but it takes just one word, or one idea, to trigger the little 'memory package' within our consciousness. Then, tumbling out of our mouth comes the belief shaped opinion, usually loaded with emotion. Suddenly we lose our openness and a closed attitude 'kicks in'. Which doesn't exactly endear us to the other as they wonder about our lack of consistency. Some time later we may even reflect and chide our self for reacting in such an opinionated and emotional way!

7 Threatened

All arguments are co-created by two or more people who each perceive themselves to be threatened. Their attachment to their belief ensures that they will 'perceive' the beliefs of the other as a personal threat. This is the root cause of all interpersonal and international conflict across the breakfast table, the corporate table and the ocean table! As a consequence fear and anger stalk the world.

8 Static

When you hold to any belief about anyone or anything then, some say, you act against the way life was meant to be. We are life energy, which is the energy of consciousness, which is dynamic and flowing. Whenever you create and hold on to any belief, consciously or subconsciously, your energy, which is you, becomes 'stuck in' the mental form that you are giving to the belief. Sometimes that can last a few moments or a few hours or many years!

Then we spend our time jumping between our beliefs like a squirrel jumping across the branches of a tree. Each time we land on an old belief we take the form of that belief and that temporarily ends our ability to flow. We get stuck playing old recordings! But it feels like familiar ground.

Belief is perhaps the deepest level at which we create a comfort zone. It gives us a false sense of support. Some say religious beliefs tend to work in this way. Beliefs are mistaken for the 'certainty of knowing', which explains many, if not most of the religious conflicts throughout history.

Viewing Point

There is a difference between an opinion and a point of view. Imagine two people one hundred yards apart looking at the same sculpture. Ask each to describe what they see and each would give a different description. They have different points of view! They are viewing the same object from different points. Which point of 'viewing' is right? Which description is right? Neither! Both points of view are neither right nor wrong. They are just different points of view.

This is essentially why there is no right or wrong in life. That's not an easy idea to embrace after a lifetime of right versus wrong 'belief conditioning'. But it doesn't give us permission to go and do anything we want. Yes that can sound like just another belief. But when you have this insight for your self that's when you no longer need to believe or not believe. You see and know ...for your self! And if you don't you are happy to say, "I don't know".

When it comes to 'material facts' e.g. someone says, "The temperature outside is 20 degrees," and then someone else says, " No it's not, it's 15 degrees". Then, when they both look at a thermometer they see it's 19 degrees. Nether was right nor wrong, they were simply 'inaccurate' in their estimation. It sounds like semantics, and to some extent it is with regard to material issues like the temperature outside. But the trap of 'right and wrong believing and thinking' is only a short step from positive and negative, then good and bad.

But within our consciousness, as we explored earlier (see Positive Thinking), there is no duality or polarity. In consciousness there is no right and wrong thinking. There is just ...thinking. There are just thoughts. Thoughts are designed to flow freely. When water is allowed to flow freely it refreshes itself. But consciousness works the other way round. Only when the constant flow of thoughts is ended does the self refresh itself. This is the effect of being in silence, of being still, within our consciousness.

When our thoughts originate out of that silence, that stillness of being, they flow naturally and easily in response to the world. But when they are shaped and flow out of our beliefs they are distorted and we keep repeating them, as if trying to prove them right.

As a result we become trapped in our thought stories. Stuck. And like water behind a damn we will stagnate and perhaps become a bit 'mentally smelly', so to speak! And we will 'feel' it!

Belief Based Opinions Generate Judgment

When we become quick to judge others thoughts and beliefs as right or wrong it's not long until we start forming beliefs about their beliefs as bad or good. That easily leads to a habit of judging the person themselves as good or bad. It's just a trap into which we have been trained to fall. But it's a trap in which we start to make our self feel some kind of unhappiness!

Then another 'inaccurate belief' kicks in, which says 'it's them that is making me feel like this'. But it's not them, it never is 'them', it's my own believing and thinking that is generating the uncomfortable and unhappy feelings. (see Responsibility)

What's the difference between an opinion and a point of view?

Opinion minus attachment to a belief equals a point of view!

When any belief is released or dissolved then what was the 'fixedness' of an opinion becomes the 'fluidity' of viewing.

When you have a 'point of view' you are aware it's not the only one. You are aware that everyone's point of view must be different because each one is looking from a different 'viewing point'! That's obvious whenever we both look outwards at something in the world with our physical eyes. But it's not so obvious when we both look at something inwardly, something in our own consciousness. We may be sharing the same words, which appear to be describing the same idea or position, but we are each creating a different perception and making a different meaning from that perception.

Many things contribute to 'meaning making' including memory, experience, already recorded beliefs, our current mood and our personal desires. We may change our physical position relative to what we are viewing externally thereby creating a new point of viewing, a new perspective.

So too, we can and likely will, change our perception of an issue if we are open to other points of view. Some people call that learning, others call it flexibility; some call it openness, while others call it common sense! But that's difficult for the person who holds to a point of view that they have hardened into a belief, which they keep trying to affirm and perhaps impose opinionatedly on others!

The reality of life is that everything is always changing in the world around us. The same applies to the world within us, the world of our consciousness. Thoughts and perceptions change, perspectives and attitudes change. So it's inevitable that life invites us to stay free within, to hold fast to no opinion, to no belief.

Being open and fluid, flexible and malleable, tend to be the foundation of a life that is lived insightfully and wisely. Perhaps that's why we tend to find the wisest of the wise live outside the constraints of any one particular 'belief system'!

How about you? Are you a compulsive believer or an open book?

What are the ten primary beliefs that you sense you hold on to?

When was the last time you co-created an argument? What particular belief were you defending and/or what belief were you attacking?

What would your life look like if you held no fixed beliefs and were prepared to 'see' from any new point of view?

What does curiosity mean to you?

ATTRACTION

BEYOND BELIEF

The heart is a beautiful magnet
That emits a powerful vibration
But it's not found in your body
It's behind all your contemplations

With tremendous pulling power
It can bring you all you need
But it's potential is so weakened
When you open its gates to greed

Whenever you choose 'to want'
There'll be a reverse effect
Diminishing your magnetism
In ways you won't detect

Your light is trapped in what you 'desire'
So you cease to radiate
The magnets field, it shrinks away
And longing is your fate

There's a paradox to be found
In this process of attraction
The less you grasp and want and crave
The greater your satisfaction

When your heart is free of wanting
When you're available to give
You are at your most attractive
And you know this is how to live

This secret of this life is revealed
When you give whatever you wanted
Your hearts desire is always returned
And nothing needs to be flaunted

So give what you want
Want not what you're giving
What you need will then arrive
And finally you can start living

**Belief in, and the application of, the law of attraction
has become a popular way
to get what you want.**

**But can it bring you what you need.
Which is what you 'really' want ...deep down!**

To get what you want you have to attract it! In fact this is possibly so 'not true' that when you realize it's a myth you will likely feel much freer inside, thereby becoming more ...attractive!

Trying to be an 'attractor' usually results in unattractiveness.

This past decade has seen the Law of Attraction become big business for many people. The preachers and the teachers of this apparent law have certainly attracted many customers and their coins as reward for purveying the idea that you can learn to attract whatever you want. But 'want' is usually the word that gives the truth away.

In many if not most instances, it's not really the law of attraction; it's the law of desire. And all desire is usually arising from the desire to be happy, satisfied, contented. Can you see that? It's just that whatever or whoever does show up in your life, possibly after much attracting, which is really much desiring, cannot 'make' you happy. At least not authentically and sustainably happy.

They or it may give you some pleasure but they/it cannot bring you happiness. That has to come from within, as you now know ...don't you? (see Happiness) What's the difference between pleasure and happiness is a great question for your next cappuccino conversation!

I am surprised some clever advertising agency has not yet promoted their product with an advert that says something like "Do you realize you have attracted this advert so you can discover the next step towards your happiest moments by buying this new ...whatever".

Yet there is always a process of attraction in motion. It's called vibration. The energy of consciousness radiates outwards. Our thoughts are outward vibrations. It's entirely invisible of course. But we are able to pick up the thought vibrations from others. While we are unlikely to pick up specific thoughts in our head we do 'feel' the energy of the other. Especially from those who are close to us in our life.

This is the idea that we are all walking radiators as well as walking magnets. We even acknowledge some people as having a 'magnetic personality'. And we will sometimes sense other people are more like drains than radiators! But even drains radiate!

The magnetic personality tends to attract to themselves those who are more easily impressed and have a 'follower consciousness'. Gurus, cult and political leaders, celebrities in the world of film and sport, are all able to attract a following. Some much more than others. Many don't particularly want this kind of attention. But it comes to them anyway. Usually enabled and magnified by the instruments of the media.

Those that do want it will often become skilled at using the media to project their magneticness, so to speak! They want the attention, the applause and probably the adulation. And millions will give them what they want. But does it make them happy? Or just addicted! History is littered with those who did attract such attention becoming extremely unhappy and even violating their own health and wellbeing as a result.

There are those however who have a vibration that attracts, not because they desire the attention and approval of others. And they don't need the magnifying power of the media. They are simply being their authentic self. They are not attractive according to what they want or what they do or what they have. They are attractive according to what 'they are' within themselves. Could this be the key to understanding the real law of attraction?

You will attract according to what you are. In other words your state of being is primary. It shapes your personality, the persona that you bring to the world. That's what people see and feel and become drawn to. Lets say you have realized and live your authenticity. What would that look like?

You are not in thrall to anyone or to what they bring to you. You are the master of your own being. You don't need or want to attract anyone or anything. You already have enough because deep down you know you already 'are' enough. There is no sense of lack or absence or indeed neediness. What is within you is sufficient. So whoever is drawn to you will come away without feeling you are not dependent on them and vice versa.

So what IS it that is within me, I hear many ask! Real wealth I hear more and more people answer. But what is real wealth and what form does it take?

Real wealth, even in this material world isn't money. Money only symbolizes material wealth. Real wealth in the material world is its natural resources. It's the potential 'energy' that is found in various natural forms within mother natures parlor, such as wood and oil. They translate into money. That which can be converted into physical energy is the real wealth.

Similarly our real personal wealth are the natural resources that lie at the core of our being, often referred to as our true nature. This is the spiritual energy that is the self.

The energy of the earth takes many forms such as coal, wood and oil. So the energy of consciousness has many natural forms. We each have the ability to shape it and give it such forms. For forms read vibrations. When you give the energy of 'you' the form of love, when you vibrate and emanate as love, you make your self a source of love, a source of spiritual wealth. Similarly with joy, care, compassion, contentment and understanding - all are different forms you give to the energy of you. They are all 'forms' of love. All make up the natural wealth of your nature, everyone's nature. Though many have obviously forgotten.

When you are able to 'be in' these natural states of being you not only express and share your wealth you become naturally attractive.

Have you ever wondered why you want what you want? Why do you want? You can only ever want what is not yours. As long as you want what is not yours you will always be wanting. Simply because everything that is not you is not yours!

So why do you want, crave, desire what is not yours? Because you are carrying a belief that if you get what you want only then can you be happy, fulfilled, complete, satisfied. Who taught you that? Probably mum or dad, or your teachers, or just society at large. It was in their interests to encourage you to want. Politicians may even convince you that it's 'wanting' that really oils the wheels of the economy and therefore society, so you are doing a good service to society by wanting.

Few will notice that wanting just brings misery. And the only relief from the misery is, yes, you guessed, want some more. That's why it's never a cure. But we still haven't really answered the question 'why' do you want. Not fully anyway.

Have you ever noticed that when you do get what you want you either decide it's not what you expected, you don't want it any more or yes, this is for me, for now. Now delete the word 'for' before 'me' at the end of that last sentence and you may start to see the deepest reason why you are always wanting.

It's simple. So simple we cannot see it. It goes something like this.

When you say "I want to have or do something", you are seeking to define your self by what you believe you will have or do. You are seeking an identity in the world. But you are not, and can never be, what you have or do.

When you say, "I want that house or car", you are seeking to define your self by what you believe you will then own. You are seeking a material identity. But you are not, and can never be, what you believe you own. Obviously.

Yes, you can say, "What about wanting to eat or clothe or warm ones self?" In truth that's not the same kind of wanting. It's more like taking care of ones body. But as soon as you start to want the special food, the designer clothes etc. you cross the line from meeting physical needs to attempting to construct an identity.

When you say, "But I want to be with that person", you are seeking to define your self by who you are with. You are seeking to use them to build your sense of 'who I am'. But you are not who you are with, you are not an association.

Every time you want anything beyond your basic needs, or anyone to be special to you, you are really seeking an identity. You are seeking your self. But here is the paradox. The one and only thing that you cannot seek is your self. The one and only thing you cannot find is your self.

You are the seeker. But you cannot be sought. There is no need to seek your self. It's impossible to find your self. Only when you realize you already 'are' your self will you realize why you cannot find your self. There is no finder, finding and found.

Confused? Yes you can say it's just a trick of language. You can say you've read a thousand experiences from people who said they sought and found themselves. You can quote hundreds of books with the aim of helping you to find the real you. But none can, simply because it's impossible to lose and find your self.

Yes I know you can even flick back some pages and quote some of the things you've read in this very book that seem to indicate that you can. You can say I am contradicting my self. Language can make it 'seem' so.

But that was then and this is now!

This is the moment right now when perhaps you 'get it'.

You get that there is nothing to get! Get it?

If you do then you're free. You always were free but you learned to 'believe' and think and act otherwise.

If you 'be' beyond belief that's when you will know.

When you know, then you are way beyond the idea (the belief) of attracting and being attractive. There is no need when you are being your self. You neither need nor want anything or anyone.

Suddenly this allows you to be available for everyone.

That then makes you exceedingly attractive ...naturally!

VALUES

BEYOND BELIEF

Many say they have values
Some are certain, others less sure
But what are these 'ideas' exactly
And what are they meant to cure

Are they something that you hold
Or just think about quite often
Or an ideal that you practice
When the self is quite forgotten

Where exactly do they live
Where can they be found
They can often seem so nebulous
Just more verbal sounds

Because we have a habit
To give each one a name
They become no longer real
Just labels, all the same

Are values simply 'things'
As we seem to be alluding
Or are they more connected
To exactly what you're doing

Is 'value' just a noun
Or something that you do
Are they one more possession
Or what makes your actions true

Do you know how to value
Have you found your own way
To extend your self as you ascribe
Your love and care each day

How we see and hold each other
In our minds and in our hearts
That's where we 'do our valuing'
As we create and play our parts

**Perhaps two of the most commonly held delusions are
a) that our beliefs are also our values and
b) values are things that we possess.**

Nothing could be further from the truth?

Values are often mistaken for things that you have. For example some say, "My values are clear, I value honesty and transparency in all dealings". Many companies have highly refined 'values statements', often hanging prominently on a wall. The statement usually specifies each value, sometimes in just one word, such as respect, loyalty, service etc. In both cases there is a misguided attempt to make 'objects' of the values. But it's better than nothing!

Similarly, in politics there is much talk about 'our values', as politicians hope you will align with their values as they try to influence your vote.

This objectifying of values is also why 'values talk' is often cheap.

In truth every thing and everyone has some value. But primarily the value doesn't lie within the person or the thing being valued, it arises from and exists within 'the valuer'. That's why value is not some thing that you have, it's something you do. It's not a noun it's a verb. Value is something that you ascribe. To talk about values as 'things' is often a way to avoid the process of ascribing value. That's when we have to walk the talk i.e. demonstrate by our actions that we actually value what we say we value.

To objectify our values by giving them names is to sabotage our capacity 'to value'. We forget I am the 'valuer' and 'valuing' is what I do. In identifying and labeling our 'values' we are trying to isolate them as something separate from our self. Then, to hold them up and display them somewhere, as if they were flags or badges of honor. Hence there can often be much talk of values but not too much walking of the 'valuing talk'.

The jeweler looks at the diamond and ascribes a monetary value to the stone. The greengrocer looks at the apples and ascribes a certain monetary value per pound of apples. These are material values in the material world that are created out of the process of 'ascription'. These are values that are measured by quantities of apples and quantities of money.

In the context of what are commonly referred to as 'spiritual values' or human values, the 'valuing process', the ascribing of value, has nothing to do with quantities and everything to do with quality.

When I say. "I value you", it's a way of saying, "I care about you". But what is the 'quality' of that care. Do I care deeply or superficially? Only I know the answer to that. The quality of my caring (valuing) is also likely to vary from moment to moment. So 'to value' is a dynamic process not a static idea or concept.

If we look into the internal process of 'valuing' we may see that it's our state of being that is allowing us to ascribe value in the first place. If we are feeling grumpy and upset about something or someone, we will care (value) about them a lot less. We have sabotaged our capacity to care. In that moment we would not value them ...so much! Perhaps we might even want to see them suffer.

Whereas when we are in a loving state of being we notice that we are able to ascribe great value to others regardless of what they say or do. You can test this every day. When you are in a good mood you value (care about) others more easily than when you are angry or fearful. This provides a major clue about what gives us the ability to ascribe value at the deepest level. It's our old friend love again!

When you are in a lovefull state of being you are able to ascribe value easily and freely. In fact 'valuing' another is what love does in the context of our relationships. When you are loving you are able to value everything and everyone around you. You care. Not worry about, care about! When you are in a fearful or angry state you notice you don't really value anything. You are too busy with your emotion, with your fearfulness and the mental story from which it's arising.

Value meets Virtue!

Virtue has been described as 'love in action'. When someone sees you being kind and generous, forgiving and understanding, empathic and grateful, they are seeing different faces of love in action. They are witnessing your virtues. They may even say to you, "You are a virtuous person". Yet these are the characteristics that most would profess to 'value' in others. So it is within the spiritual energy of consciousness that virtue meets value. They are one and the same. Value is what we do from inside out. We ascribe value to others in our own consciousness. That is what leads to 'virtuous behavior' which is what people see and receive from outside in!

Take a moment and notice when your intention is to be kind to someone. This is a form of love in action. Implicit within your energy (consciousness), from the intention of kindness through to action of doing kindness, is you saying to the other 'I value you'. You are ascribing value to the other through your kindness. You can do exactly the same through all the other 'virtues'.

When you 'respect' someone you are ascribing value to that person within your consciousness first. Then, if it's authentic, it will show up in the creative process from intention to action. They will feel respected. Virtue is seen in the act of valuing.

Ascribing value is an act of love. It is love in action. If you are not in a loving state you would not be able to ascribe value very well, if at all. Not Hollywood love. I say that just because of the baggage we often associate with love tends to be limited by the idea of romantic love. But that is seldom love and more often desire, attachment and dependency. When these 'impulses' are present within a relationship the capacity to value the other tends to make frequently quick exits from our consciousness.

So why do we find it so hard so often to value another person. The main reason is belief. It's our beliefs that sabotage our ability to value, to care for another, to respect the other, to understand the other. We all seem to be carrying certain beliefs that get in the way of our ability to walk the talk of valuing.

Lets say one of your key values is respect. But as soon as you create the belief, usually in a form of judgment, that, "They are not a good person", in any way, you lose the ability to ascribe (give) respect. Whereas the person who is able to be respectful in all situations in all relationships will never create a 'judgmental belief' about the other, ever! Easy eh!

You may say you value 'co-operation' but if you are carrying the 'belief' that competition is a good thing and necessary for progress then, at some stage, that belief will block and distort your ability to be co-operative. You will not be able to value the other or the relationship in a way that allows you to co-operate with the other.

In the workplace especially, this can become the leaders greatest challenge. They want to build a culture of co-operation within the team but the marketplace outside the context of the team relationships runs on rampant competition. This is why it's not easy for a commercial organization to bring the values they identify as important to life within the culture of the organization. Eventually they will run into a values/beliefs clash.

You may say 'trust' is an essential value to your relationships. But as soon as you 'believe' that what 'they' said or did hurt 'me' you will withdraw your trust and no longer be able to walk that talk. Until of course you realize that no one hurts your feelings. That's just a belief we all learned as children. At the mental/emotional level we are the creator of our 'hurt feelings', always. (see Responsibility)

Increasingly compassion is a common value in many cultures. But we will not be able to be compassionate the moment we create the belief that 'they deserve what they get' or 'they had it coming'.

In so many ways our beliefs sabotage our values. This is why we so often see a contradiction in people's words and actions. But you can't blame them. The beliefs they are carrying, and the habits of re-emerging those beliefs into behavior, is so deep and so strong they themselves often don't see their own contradiction. It's an invitation to your understanding and compassion for them! If you blame them in any way then you are re-creating the belief that you are a victim!

Values and not Beliefs

We also tend to get our beliefs and values mixed up. It seems some of us believe that beliefs and values are the same. But they're not.

Beliefs tend to be static ideas and concepts we create, record and use to shape our mindset, our thinking ...without thinking! Valuing is dynamic and fluid, arising from our heart, the heart of our being. But only when our heart is clear of all obstructions i.e. without attachment to anything or anyone including our beliefs!

When we convert dynamic process of 'valuing' into static concepts about values that's when they tend to become beliefs. Ironically when we make beliefs out of our values that's what gets in the way of being able 'to value'.

Which brings us to another common confusion between our values and our attachments. I may say I value my car. But if it is damaged and I become upset in any way, then I wasn't valuing the car, I was attached to it. When you are attached to anything or anyone you cannot value them or it. Why, because attachment generates fear of loss and the anger of blame. Fear means we are contracted and self-absorbed, which are internal conditions that stop us from expanding and extending care (value) to others.

We tend to say 'we value' when we really mean we are 'attached'. But we are not aware we are mixing the two. How about you? To what or to whom do you say, "I value that/you", but deep down know you are attached?

Exit Truth enter Belief

Beliefs are what we create when we lose awareness of what is true. The main sign of this is when we talk of what we seek. We don't notice that whatever we seek is what has been lost. It was once known, otherwise we would not know what to seek. For example, we may talk a lot about the need for respect and how there should be respect for each other. In other words we are seeking respect. Understandably, as it's the foundation of harmonious human relationships and because it so often appears to be absent.

We believe our relationships should be built on respect but don't realize whenever we are criticizing, complaining or blaming another we are contradicting our self. Yet we know, deep down, that mutual respect is the true way forward. But we tend not to walk that talk when it is held just as a belief.

To restore the truth of respect in our relationships means having a completely different vision of the other and that starts with having a completely different vision of ones self.   And that, as they say, is not as easy as popping into your local cafe for another cappuccino!

So watch what you say you value. Do you really?

And are you able to maintain your 'valuing' consistently without your beliefs getting in the way?

Contemplate and discuss, curiously explore, and clarity will ensue.

SPIRITUALITY

BEYOND BELIEF

It's such an ancient mystery
What it is and where it's found
Does it live inside somewhere
Or is it felt to be all around

You can't see it with your eyes
It can't be captured in a box
It's invisible and intangible
But it's as real as your socks

Defined by your state of being
It's your authenticity
It expresses as your nature
But only when you're free

All the ancients recommended
That to know your self as spirit
Is to awaken from the dream
See your ego and then kill it

If you can sit so quietly
And watch what's passing through
You'll notice that you're not your mind
And nothing's happening to YOU

If you become so very still
You will know the power you are
You will sense the beauty of just being
And your real home is not far

Then all those nagging questions
Like who am I, what is me
Dissolve without an answer
Allowing you just to be

To be or not to be
Is not the question to ask
But to be the being you already are
It's not just another task

You probably believe that spirit is some mysterious energy that inhabits some part of your body or that it's all around and everywhere.

It's neither and both!

"I am a spiritual person", is a self-description often used by those who believe they are. But it's often an ideal that is aspired to, rather than an honest description of ones self.

Few people seem to ask, "But what does 'spiritual person' really mean? What does spirituality really mean?" For some it means being interested in things of the spirit, which may just involve reading books categorized as spiritual. For others it means being kind and compassionate and having good intentions. For many it means integrating some so called spiritual practices into their life. And for others it means some form of what is often categorized as 'spiritualism', and that can range from anything from tarot cards to hypnotism, from crystal healing to a hundred other different therapies. All of which are frequently found in one place otherwise known as Mind Body Spirit festivals!

Such festivals of apparent spirituality tend to be signs that the true meaning of spirituality has been lost in the mists of time and many belief systems. There is now a kind of liberty to put almost anything under this umbrella term. When people encounter any of the above under the label 'spiritual' it's similar to following a sign on the road that actually leads nowhere. But you don't know it leads nowhere until you arrive at ...nowhere. That's the moment you realize what you believed was spiritual ...isn't really! But that can take a very long time. In the meantime whatever road you do follow will always take you where you are meant to be!

So what is spirituality? The starting point is spirit itself. Almost all ancient wisdoms (but seldom religions) remind us that spirituality begins with the realization that it's not some mysterious, holy or mythical energy working invisibly in the background of life. It is not some unknown entity that occupies a part of your body. It is what I am. It is the energy of consciousness itself. It's not that you have a spirit it's that you 'are' spirit. Many words are loosely used to describe it like soul, psyche, self, being, I etc.

Science has a problem with all of that simply because this energy is non-physical and therefore non-tangible, and cannot be captured, seen and examined in a scientific way. The 'effects' of the presence and the activity of spirit/self can be observed but not the energy itself. Many fields of science believe they are approaching the moment of revelation, when spirit or the soul is proved to exist ...scientifically. But from a purely scientific standpoint, which requires material 'proof by test tube and scalpel', it's likely to always remain in the realms of 'impossible to prove the existence of spirit'.

That's why we have mystics. They are the real spiritual scientists, hard at work in their own laboratory known as consciousness. You, I, we, are all mystics when we decide to 'see for our self'. Not with physical eyes but with the eye of awareness.

You could say that every experience you have is a spiritual experience simply because it's you, the spiritual being, that is experiencing. But what is the 'quality' of the experience. What is felt, seen and known within the experience, which is really an 'insperience'?

Few people, it seems, can answer that question for two reasons. We haven't developed the language, nor the practice of putting into language, exactly what is occurring within our consciousness, within our self as spirit. That's because we are generally just not very aware of what is occurring within our consciousness. This requires the deliberate cultivation of an inner awareness, which is not commonly taught by parents or teachers.

Being authentically spiritual begins with and is founded on the realization that spirit is what I am. That's what is often missing in the many 'activities/therapies' etc. that are positioned under the umbrella of spirituality. That's because it's not an easy 'aha' moment to induce. It's also quite challenging to sustain and then allow it to alter our mindset. But if the self fully realizes spirit/soul is what I am, it kind of changes ...everything!

So why is it not easy to sustain such an awareness? Simply because we are all taught to 'believe' we are only the form that we see in the mirror. This leads to mistakenly believing that sensual experience i.e. physical stimulation, is the only way to know and feel love and happiness.

We don't notice that it's the belief we are only a material form that generates the emotion of fear. Fear of loss, fear of not getting, not feeling, what I want. Fear of others doing what I don't want. So fear, in one of its forms, becomes the main sign that we are asleep to who we are as a being of spiritual energy.

When you know your self as spirit/soul and you can sustain that awareness you have no fear. You have nothing to lose. There is nothing that you want. You are no longer interested in what others are doing. It's their business. Unless it's very close to home and you are in the same room. In which case you might seek to understand them, or help them, or guide them, or support them.

Where there is fear and indeed any emotional disturbance you are not being spiritual. You are being emotional. Unfortunately we are so unaware of the true nature of our emotions. We are so addicted to some emotions that we are not aware we are not being spiritual. This unawareness is also what allows so many therapies to give themselves the label of spiritual. They believe being emotional is the same as being spiritual.

What do you think?

Is that true for you? Do you believe it or know it?

The disturbance of emotion interferes with the clarity of our intellect and skews both our decisions and our thoughts. Emotion arises from attachment, which is code for 'that's mine' which is the first symptom of selfishness. Authentic spirituality is entirely unselfish. Would you agree? Spirituality is non emotional. Is that true? Love is not an emotion but the word we use to describe the highest vibration of consciousness.

We can only be our self, as spirit itself, when we are fully free within our self. That means no attachment to anything or anybody. No dependency on anything or anyone. No desire for anything or anyone. This, for most, is hard to conceive never mind embody. Such is our conditioning, and such is the world at this time, that attachment, dependency and desire are the currency of almost all our relationships to some degree or other.

What do you think?

Only when attachment and dependency is no more, can we allow the purity of our own natural state of being in the form of contentment, lovefulness, and that 'joie de vivre' that lives in everyone's heart, come to the surface. Only then, when we have no agenda in our relationships i.e. want nothing from no one, can our intentions towards others be truly benevolent, therefore truly spiritual.

True or false? What does spirituality mean to you?

Being spiritual is a natural expression of 'being spirit' and not trying to be anything or anyone else. There is a quality of innocence that can only come with the end of all judgment and criticism. There is an unshakable intention to be there for the other but not to pander or indulge the other.

Being spiritual recognizes the other as a spiritual being and there is no longer the impulse to label the other in any way.

Unconditional acceptance, continuous appreciation and a childlike gratitude are the gifts that the spiritual person brings to all their relationships.

How would you describe spirituality as in 'being spiritual'?

GOD

BEYOND BELIEF

We seek HIM here
We seek HER there
We just can't find IT
Anywhere

It's as if we sense a presence
Intuitively some know
There is one who's above us all
Who never makes a show

Many claim special access
An exclusive 'in' you see
But they never present the evidence
Of HIS existence or reality

So how are we to tell
If SHE's with us all the time
In what ways can we know
Like our parents, forever mine

Many Gods have come and gone
Is there one that stays behind
Is there a God here for us all
Or is it all just in the mind

Do you have to join a group
With their tailor-made beliefs
Or can you know just by your self
And request your sins relief

They say be still and know I am
Is the mystical way to connect
With our oldest friend and lover
Who gives and then forgets

Perhaps there is no answer
To who or what is HE
Is SHE the ultimate nobody
Yet the only ONE that's free

It's up to you to see
For yourself to feel and know
Otherwise you'll get sucked in
To many wondrous Godly shows

Have you been taught to believe in God?
Or to believe there is no God?
Either way it's still just a belief.

And that's what's 'in the way'!

Often in public talks I ask for a show of hands from all those who 'believe' in God. On average 70 to 80 per cent will raise their hands. And that's precisely the problem! (not forgetting there are no Problems!) Is God just a belief? That's what you make God into when you believe.

Is your mother a belief? Is your child a belief? Is your best friend a belief? Is the sun in the sky a belief? Do you believe they exist? Obviously 'no' to all of those questions, simply because you 'know' them. You have a direct personal connection and relationship with each. That's because you can see them and even physically feel them by touching them or letting them touch you.

Now this is where things get a little tricky. Do you know that you exist? Many would say, "Of course I do because I can see my hands moving. I can see myself in the mirror. I feel physical pain". But what if you are, as has been frequently suggested in this and a thousand other books, a non-physical being. What if you are that non-material entity called 'spirit or soul'? Do you know that you exist as a non-material entity, as a conscious being i.e. a being of consciousness?

Well that could be another belief unless and until you 'insperience' your self as being non-material. How? By being aware that there is a non-material universe within you. That universe is comprised of non-material things like thoughts, feelings, perceptions, emotions memories etc. These are 'events' in consciousness. These are your creation and if the creation is non-material it's likely the creator, by necessity, is also non-material. That's why, for thousands of years, the practices of meditation and contemplation have been the foundation of spirituality and spiritual awakening. In other words they are the ways to realize and know your self as a spiritual being, a non-material entity!

They are, in their simplest forms, practices to remind you that you are not made of material; you are not of this material world. You are what is sometimes referred to as the ghost in the machine. The soul in the body.

Now, if you/I/we, are non-material in essence, it's likely that the being we call God is also the same. Here is perhaps why so few know god and simply carry their own belief about him/her/it. They create and carry their own version of him/her/it. If you don't BE the non-material being you will not be able to connect with and recognize another being who is non-material.

A blind person in a room of people is not able to see and know of any others in the room. But if they are told others are in the room they will then create the belief that others are present. They will then create speculative beliefs about what they are like. But they still don't 'know' until they hear or touch the others. At which point they can 'feel' directly, the presence of those others. Then they will start to know their personalities.

Now lets apply that as a metaphor to our unawareness and/or ignorance about the presence of God or a supreme/perfect intelligence or whatever label you prefer to give to that 'being'.

If it's been realized that the self is non-material i.e. spiritual energy, then it's likely the supreme intelligence is also non-material i.e. spiritual energy. So we could never 'feel' it's presence at a physical level i.e. through ears and hands, and certainly not eyes. Yet we also do 'feel' at a subtle and non-material level.

Feeling is described as 'perception by touch'. Subtle feelings are when you feel the subtle energy or presence of another. You perceive the energy they are emitting. You pick up their vibration and describe it as something you feel. It's entirely non-material. In an intimate relationship with another human being we develop the ability to feel their energy. We can instantly sense what mood they are in because we have been so close to them for so long. With some people we seem able to do this from a distance.

This is perhaps the only way to feel the presence of the being called God or the supreme spirit, soul, intelligence, please use your own label/title. ITS emanations/vibrations are likely to be of the highest vibration simply because IT is the supreme intelligence or, as some would describe, the purest being. It would therefore follow that in order for us to 'feel and know' that presence we would need to be in the same 'vibratory state'. We would need to be in a subtle state where we could feel that subtle energy in order to be aware of ITS subtle presence.

At a physical level it's a bit like your body's relationship with the sun. You don't need to see the sun to know its presence. You can close your eyes and 'feel' the sun over your whole body. Until clouds get in the way and suddenly you lose that warming feeling. Or if you wear lots of clothes you obviously won't 'feel' the sun on your whole body.

Unsurprisingly, feeling the subtle spiritual energy of the 'spiritual sun' is challenging for human beings. We have become so accustomed to being/vibrating at such a lower level, the material level, simply because we make the mistake of believing we are just a material form.

When we carry that belief then almost the only vibrations we are aware of, indeed interested in, are material ones. Sensual ones. Ones that come from 'outside in', through our physical senses. That would be at a much lower vibratory level than the subtle state of pure consciousness.

This may explain (only explain!) why so few can back up their claim to 'know' God. They believe there is a God. They believe in the idea of God. But they don't know for sure. To believe is to say, "I don't know". They don't know because they have not raised their vibration, there state of being, enough to feel the subtle presence of the spiritual sun.

How would you know if someone knew Him/Her/IT for sure? This is such a good question. One answer maybe this. If God is the purest and highest spiritual intelligence then to make that personal connection with that being you would also have to be able to be at that highest, purest vibratory state of consciousness.

Down here in the material world of material descriptions, that state would probably be called 'pure love'. If such a human being had been able to cultivate that state of being, and be in it consistently, then, in the presence of that human being, you and I would probably feel their vibration and be affected, touched, in some way. We would probably feel uplifted by it. Unless of course you and I were vibrating at such a low level we would be incapable of feeling it in that moment. We would be oblivious to their elevated vibration.

It seems most of us are vibrating at such a low level we are not capable of feeling and knowing directly the presence of, well, you know who! What keeps us at that low level? Yes, you guessed, our old friend belief.

The beliefs that I am just a physical entity, that the material world out there is the primary reality, that physical stimulation is the only way to happiness, that becoming attached to another physical form is the only way to find love, that ...well, we could go on, but I would just be repeating all the beliefs in this book so far.

These beliefs are like the clothing of our consciousness. They stop us from 'feeling' the warmth of the spiritual sun on and in our being. Beliefs make us blind. We cannot see, which means we cannot feel the subtle presence of HIS/HER much higher vibration so we cannot know IT actually exists. So we settle for a 'belief in' ...IT.

Then we become attached to our belief in our God, get together with those who share the same belief, and when it is not shared by others we might go to war! Sorry, that was a quick jump. But the history of religion tends to point that way. Whereas the history of authentic spirituality tends to point towards those few who are free of belief. They have emptied their consciousness thereby raising the vibration of their consciousness and reconnected with that pure and perfect subtle presence for themselves. So they say!

For those who hold the spiritual source, God, the divine One, the supreme intelligence, just as a belief, it means there must be some doubt. But better not to let anyone else see or hear such doubting. They think, "Better not to let them think I am not a person of belief or faith". And so the ego enters and sits at the center of their ideas about God. Perhaps they have not yet realized the ego is created at the exact moment they attach to and build their identity out of their belief about their God.

They have also not yet realized that it's the ego that stops them being beyond belief and being able to create a personal connection with 'the source'.

Oh well! It's obviously what is meant to be. Would you agree?

Otherwise it would not be this way.

So in conclusion, not forgetting there are no conclusions (see Conclusion) if you want to connect with and 'know' Him/Her/IT you will have to kill your 'belief' in God!

You will have to kill ALL your beliefs about, everything and everyone! Just a small task, before breakfast.

It's probably not an idea that would go down too well in churches, temples and mosques throughout the land!

In the reality of you, if and when you meditate, you are in fact withdrawing your light, your energy, your attention, from ALL the beliefs you hold within your consciousness.

This is what allows them to die a slow death.

This is what allows you to awaken and be beyond belief.

And that's exactly what makes you a killer

...of beliefs!

DREAMING

BEYOND BELIEF

So you think it's real
This world you perceive
But have you ever challenged
What you were taught to believe

The first thing to notice
Is that you create
Your version of this life
According to your state

If you ask the question
What exactly shapes your vision
You will likely notice
Your beliefs in collision

So how should you interpret
What's in front of you
How should you perceive
To see what is true

You will likely realize
Your beliefs are like a matrix
Shaping your perceptions
Your inner conjurer's tricks

Beliefs are simply memories
Ideas and images past
Like dreams they're re-awoken
In awareness they never last

But if that's what you use
To create your version of now
You may as well be dreaming
Not knowing why or how

It's really hard to fathom
How life is but a dream
You may believe you know
But nothing's as it seems

**You have been clearly taught to believe that
whatever you see is real.
Yes, you guessed!**

It usually isn't, in the truest sense of the word.

There are some wisdom paths that assert that life is just a dream. That what you see around you is not real. At least not as real as you believe. Some spiritual and philosophical viewpoints even go as far as to say it's all an illusion. But what do they mean exactly?

It's probably best summed up by the old saying 'two men looked out from their prison cell, one saw prison bars and other just saw the stars'. Our perception is our reality. What we perceive is what is real for each of us. While there are events taking place in the material world of people and situations, only our perception of such events is truly, personally real.

That said, even that reality is a dream.

Everything you see and bring into your mind through physical eyes goes through your own personal filter. As we now know that filter is made up of your beliefs and past experiences.

Let's say you learned to believe that other human beings are all nasty and dangerous. You will then filter and interpret everyone around you as potentially nasty and dangerous. It's obviously not true, not real, that everyone is nasty and dangerous all the time. But lets say you believe they are. So you create them that way within you, according to your belief. Your creation is then like a dream. It's not reality, as most people are not nasty and dangerous. Yet the dream is real for you. That's what dreaming means when you are physically awake.

You are misperceiving the world around you according to your beliefs and memories. As long as you allow your beliefs and memories to be your filter of the world you will never see the world as it truly is, or others as they truly are. You will dream them. They are there in front of you but your creation, your version of them, will be what you see, what you dream. It seems real to you as you are not aware you are doing this.

As soon as you begin to integrate any introspective practice like meditation or contemplation into your life, you will start to notice this. If you're interested then your curiosity will be aroused. It may start in a small ways at first. For example, a conversation about a film you watched with friends. You start to notice that while you all watched the same film you all saw different things. At some point someone may even say, "Were we all watching the same movie".

You saw the movie but as you watched it you filtered it. You re-created it according to your perception. And the primary component of your perception is your already created beliefs.

The only way to see the world and other people without dreaming them i.e. to see everything clearly and cleanly, is to have no beliefs and therefore no memories. Possible? Mmm!

Lets dig a little deeper into that question. It's really asking can you live your life without believing in anything. Can you have no beliefs? What an interesting enquiry to finish the book, he said believingly! The answer could be yes. But I have to be honest and say I don't know. But another cliche comes to mind. If you can conceive it, you can achieve it.

If you can conceive of the possibility that you can live without belief then it can become a reality. What do you think? By saying no, it's not possible to live without belief, then we instantly limit our self. We are saying don't even explore to see if it's possible. That's like the climbers of Mount Everest getting to base camp and saying, "This is nice here. Lets just stay here and enjoy the view". By saying, "Yes, it may be possible to live beyond belief, but I don't yet know how or what or why exactly", I throw down the gauntlet to myself.

Now I need to look deeply into my own consciousness to see if such a state of being can exist, has ever existed. If it has existed I need to see if that state may still be there within me. Before I do it out loud on these pages may I recommend you take a moment to close the book and ask your self the same question. Can you live your life without belief?

If so what would that look like? What would that mean? Contemplate and ruminate for a moment. Start a conversation. Enquire curiously.

In day-to-day life we make many assumptions. Assumptions are really beliefs. I assume (believe) you will get me the information I need. I assume (believe) the chair will hold my weight. I assume (believe) the train will arrive on time. I assume (believe) the sun will rise once again. Now we all know what happens when we make assumptions, which are really just beliefs in disguise. At some point our assumption will not be fulfilled. Because we held the assumptions as beliefs to which we became attached we will be extremely disappointed when the chair will break, the train is late, the other person forgets and the bank goes bust etc.

We will then project our disappointment onto the situation or person or organizations. And then carry on making the same assumptions/beliefs. This is what is really meant to live in a dream like state while physically awake. Unless we realize it's possible to stop making assumptions i.e. creating such beliefs.

Let's say you fully accept the fact that chairs sometimes break, trains are sometimes late, people don't always do what they say and banks sometimes go bust. That means you are no longer attached to such assumptions/beliefs. So you no longer suffer when such events actually happen.

By letting go and moving away, moving beyond all such beliefs, you are taking your self beyond disappointment, anger and fear. You are making suffering impossible. Reality reminds us that all such things can and will happen in the world out there. We have developed the habit of creating and holding beliefs that are in contradiction to that reality. Until we realize we are arguing with reality we will keep arguing and never win.

Can you see it? Now expand that idea, that principle, out into daily life. You will soon start to notice all your moments of any kind of unhappiness are entirely due to your unmet assumptions/beliefs. You will also notice that as soon as you drop the belief you will start to 'know' with great clarity all that may or may not happen. Or putting the egg before the chicken, when you fully realize (know) that anything can happen that is NOT according to any belief, you start to see the folly of creating and attaching to such beliefs in the first place.

So it makes sense not to create assumptions/beliefs about anything. If you do then you will never be disappointed, angry or sad. You will never be unhappy with anything or anyone. And yet you would still be fully engaged with everything and everyone. In fact more deeply engaged as you are no longer be distracted by the emotions that arise from unmet assumptions/beliefs.

So it is possible to live without creating beliefs about almost everything. But it's not easy to get from here to there. But if you can see the possibility in theory first you may be glimpsing a level of freedom you didn't know existed, until now.

So when things do go unexpectedly, they don't! Nothing is unexpected any more. Everything is just going. With that awareness you start to see the world as it really is and people as they really are in each and every moment.

But wait, that only covers the third level of reality i.e. beliefs about what is going on in the material world around you 'out there'.

Then there are the beliefs about the intangible, non-physical, 'second reality' aspects of life. This is the reality of your consciousness and the continuous stream of events 'in here'. Is it possible to live without belief about and within this context? Some would say it's not only possible it's an absolute necessity. In fact if you glance back through this book you will see almost all the beliefs are essentially of a non-tangible internal nature. If only because that's where all beliefs are created, sustained and held.

They are mostly to do with what's going on in your consciousness. They are all beliefs that cause some kind of stress, sorrow or suffering within oneself. Why? First, because they are not true. Second, we have a tendency to become attached to our beliefs without the awareness that we are attached to them.

They exist in our consciousness because we have not yet realized that, "I believe because I don't know". Beliefs are therefore a form of ignorance!

It's only by realizing and saying 'I don't know' that the seeing of deeper truths becomes possible. As you do these beliefs then cease to influence your creation of perception, thought and feeling. They atrophy naturally. Some die slowly others instantly.

The only way to kill your beliefs, and therefore your attachment to your illusions, is with the realization of what is true, with the 'seeing' and knowing of what is real.

That starts with a confession, "I am ignorant as I do not know if that is true". Yet!

The moment you realize this you have begun your journey to the land beyond belief.

What else is there to do but to see and be beyond belief?

May you see for your self with brilliant clarity.

So WHO are YOU... really?

So finally, when all is said and done, and you have reached that place beyond belief, one question remains...

Who are you ...really? Are you sitting comfortably? The following text may trigger some discomfort. It won't 'make' you uncomfortable but it may 'trigger' some mental/emotional agitation. In other words you may 'make your self' feel uncomfortable as you read. But then again you may not.

It's just words remember!

How you convert such words into 'meaning' will be unique to you. You will create your own version of what you are about to read according to the beliefs you are already holding. It's those beliefs that will define your comfort and/or discomfort levels.

Can you change your beliefs? Of course you can. Perhaps you used to believe the world was flat but now you believe it's round. Or the other way round! OK, so you already always believed it was round. Let's try another. Perhaps you used to believe that your happiness was something to be found in the world, or from other people, but now you believe (perhaps you know) your happiness is something that arises from within you. It's your job to create it.

So who does the changing? You do! So there is YOU and there are your beliefs. Even logic then says YOU are not your beliefs!

So are you a Muslim a Christian a Jew a Buddhist or an anything? No? Because they are just beliefs! You didn't come out of the womb with Muslim or Christian or Buddhist or anything stamped on you forehead. One day someone just said, "You are a Christian, or a Muslim or a Jew etc", and you just blindly believed them. Then they said it again and again. Why? Because they believed what their parents and community told them. They believed they are their beliefs. But they are not and YOU are not a belief.

Just as your body is not what's in the shopping bag you are carrying home, YOU are not the beliefs you hold and carry in your consciousness.

The same goes for your nationality. Did you arrive with I am French or I am Syrian or I am Canadian carved into some body part. Nooo! It's just a label. Which is just another belief. And YOU are not a belief! You create them and you sustain them, or not, as the case may be. But YOU are not them!

Those big people called adults have just convinced us to create our sense of 'who I am' out of a belief and then expand that into a belief system. Why? Because they learned to do the same when they were young and innocent. They also ...just believed!

So how many beliefs have you learned to use to build your sense of 'who I am'? Religion, nationality, race, profession, age, fashion, looks, possessions, the list is long. Even believing you are the gender of your body is just a belief. That's why some boys are more girlie than girls. And vice versa!

Your body has gender but YOU don't!

When you buy a fashion item because you like the style or the brand, you create a belief, "This is like me, this is how I want to be seen, this is me". Sometimes you even think, "I can identify with this or I want to be identified as this". Sometimes friends even stand with us watching us try on new clothes saying, "Yes that's definitely you!". Suddenly your belief about who you are is based on the style of a piece of clothing or the brand label on the clothing.

Can you see they are ALL just beliefs. And YOU are not a belief. I am not a belief. We are not beliefs! When you begin to see this clearly you will start to awaken. Until then, yes, you are asleep. Beliefs are like sleeping pills for our awareness. This is why 99.9999 per cent of the human race is sleepwalking through their life.

Amazing isn't it?

But remember! Don't believe me!

OK let's do this another way. You pick up a book. Let's say it's what we call a scripture. You absorb the information. It's just information in the material form of words. But you use it to create beliefs, non-material ideas, in your consciousness. Then you build your identity out of those beliefs. You start to look at the world and other people through your beliefs. Lo and behold, it's no wonder you start to judge many of those people not only as weirdly different but as a threat! You may even get together with others who have built their identity out of similar beliefs using the same information as you and go to war! Why? Because you believe you are your beliefs! You are however, not aware of this. You have no idea you are fast asleep!

Yes you're awake, but you're asleep!

Then you thread your beliefs into stories. Personal stories of 'my' life. Stories of 'my' relationships. Stories about 'my' job. Stories about, well anything. "Let me tell you 'my story'", we say to each other over coffee each day. Or let me tell you some biblical stories, or koranic stories, or some budhistic stories. But it's not YOU. It's just a story. And YOU are not a story. It's just a story made up by someone else, out of a thousand beliefs and adopted by you. And you and I and we, are not 'beliefs'.

Wake up!

So that brings us to the big question, if you are not your beliefs then who are you?   "Who am I?" you may ask. And many do. Then they wonder why there is no satisfying answer! Why there is no, "Aha! Of course, that's who I am". Any answer just becomes another belief. And beliefs are just like mist, like fog, like clouds in the sky. They have no substance. And they are always changing their form. Eventually they all disappear. But YOU never disappear.

You are prior to all beliefs, prior to any 'idea' about who you are, which means prior to all thinking and thoughts. Prior to any event in your consciousness, in you. You are pure consciousness. Like the sky behind and beyond the clouds. It's always there but it is never confused with the clouds. But right now you're not so pure because you have polluted your self, your consciousness, with yes, you guessed, beliefs! The clouds of your beliefs are obscuring the clarity of you the sky.

Now please don't start thinking. "Well surely it's OK if my beliefs are positive". All beliefs are viruses in consciousness that will distort your ability to perceive with absolute clarity and accuracy. Any and all beliefs are prisons in which we trap our self thus relinquishing our freedom. Yes this is where our freedom goes. Lost in a jungle of beliefs in our own head. This is why we become confused. But of course we are not aware we do so. In fact, even if we do become aware, there's a belief waiting to console us and let us off the hook, and it sounds like, "Well it's natural to have and to hold and identify with such beliefs, it's human nature, everyone does, so it must be OK".

This really is the sign we have fallen into the BIG sleep!

Can you see it? Just see. Don't believe or not believe. Just see if you can see this for your self. Look gently. Without force. Without tension. Not only will you start to 'see' this for your self you will notice you are seeing with greater clarity. You will be left with one question and one question only.

Who is doing the 'seeing'?

YOU are. The one who is no longer holding and looking 'through' any beliefs. You see with clarity because you are free of belief. Freedom for a human being is no longer using beliefs to interpret other people's actions and attitudes or indeed anything in the world. It's called innocence. But it's not a helpless childlike innocence. It's a wise innocence, a quietly strong innocence, a pure innocence. An innocence that knows!

But please don't make the mistake of just believing this. Sit, be quiet, be aware, be curious, and just be. And you will see.

You may even start to laugh. Chuckle perhaps, as you realize the foolish mistake of building a sense of 'who I am' out of a set of beliefs given to you by someone else. You will certainly realize there is no such human being known as a Christian, as a Muslim, as a Jew, as Spanish, as Italian etc. They are illusions we create about our self and then build a story out of and around such illusions. Tradition, culture and religion follows.

Then you will notice how you've done the same with fashion, possessions, titles, positions, professions, possessions etc. The more you see and realize your own self-made illusions about your self the more you will notice your self 'becoming' freer and freer. You feel it first. You feel its authenticity. As you do you are restoring your own authenticity. Others will notice you being more authentic as it starts to affect everything you say and do.

All because you notice, that in reality, YOU are not your beliefs. You are no one. How's that for a paradox? To be your self it is necessary to realize you are no one!

There will be a period when you will swing between trying to be someone, as you run your stories filled with beliefs in your mind, and being no one, the one who has realized I am not my beliefs therefore the stories are not about me!

The more you give attention to just watching, observing, how you build your sense of 'who I am' out of the beliefs you create, the more you will realize how ridiculous it is and stop doing it. It's not usually one moment and your out and free. For most people it's a process. A gradual, progressive inner walk back to authenticity, clarity and freedom.

There is no hurry. The more you try to hurry this the more time and energy it will take. This is why meditation and contemplation are so useful as practices to build into your life. With such practices you will notice your habit of imprisoning your self in a set of beliefs, hundreds of times every day.

Only then can you, will you, restore your own freedom. Only then will you see that YOU are not who or what you believed you are.

Only then will to see that you are just the one who is seeing.

You are seeing itself.

Don't believe.

See!

What to DO!

1

If you want to see and understand with pristine
clarity be not attached to any belief.

2

If you want to be free then recognize and drop all
the beliefs you are using to trap your 'self'.

3

If you would like to cultivate your appreciation of 'the subtle' then
you, your self, will need to become subtle,
not as a belief but as a reality.

4

If you feel it's time for greater honesty just keep saying,
"I don't know", the ego won't like it
but you will, eventually.

5

If you would like to rediscover your capacity to love
and to know the greatest happiness,
stop 'believing' in both.

6

Some small confidence may arise out of believing
but super-confidence arises out of knowing,
especially knowing that 'I don't know'.
Unbelievable, isn't it?

7

If you want to 'know' you will have to
leave all your 'beliefs' behind.

With which belief will YOU begin?

Mike George frequently writes, speaks, guides, facilitates, leads and
coaches and, as you now know, helps people turn
their world upside down and their
thinking inside out.

www.mikegeorgebooks.com

www.relax7.com

or email

mike@relax7.com

CPSIA information can be obtained
at www.ICGtesting.com
Printed in the USA
FSHW02n1541120618
49057FS

9 780993 387722